ACADEMIC WORD POWER 4

ACADEMIC WORD POWER 4

Barbara Jones

Series editor: Donna Obenda
University of North Texas

Houghton Mifflin Company
Boston ■ New York

Editor in Chief: *Patricia A. Coryell*
Director of ESL Publishing: *Susan Maguire*
Senior Development Editor: *Kathleen Sands-Boehmer*
Editorial Assistant: *Evangeline Bermas*
Cover Design Manager: *Diana Coe*
Marketing Manager: *Annamarie Rice*

Printed in the U.S.A.

Library of Congress Control Number: 2003103472

ISBN: 0-618-39774-4

1 2 3 4 5 6 7 8 9 - POO - 07 06 05 04 03

CONTENTS

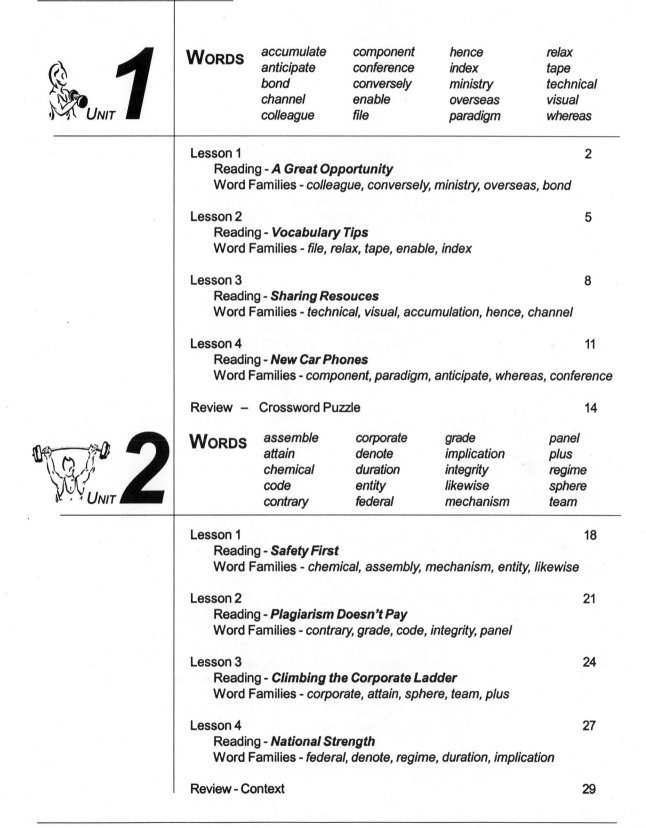

3 UNIT

WORDS

appendix	compound	ethical	medium
arbitrary	contact	facilitate	ongoing
bulk	diminish	founded	portion
chart	encounter	insight	reluctant
classical	expansion	mature	temporary

4 UNIT

WORDS

adjacent	currency	inherent	preliminary
analogy	deviate	manual	revolution
cease	enormous	nonetheless	rigid
coincide	erode	norm	supplement
convince	format	overlap	undergo

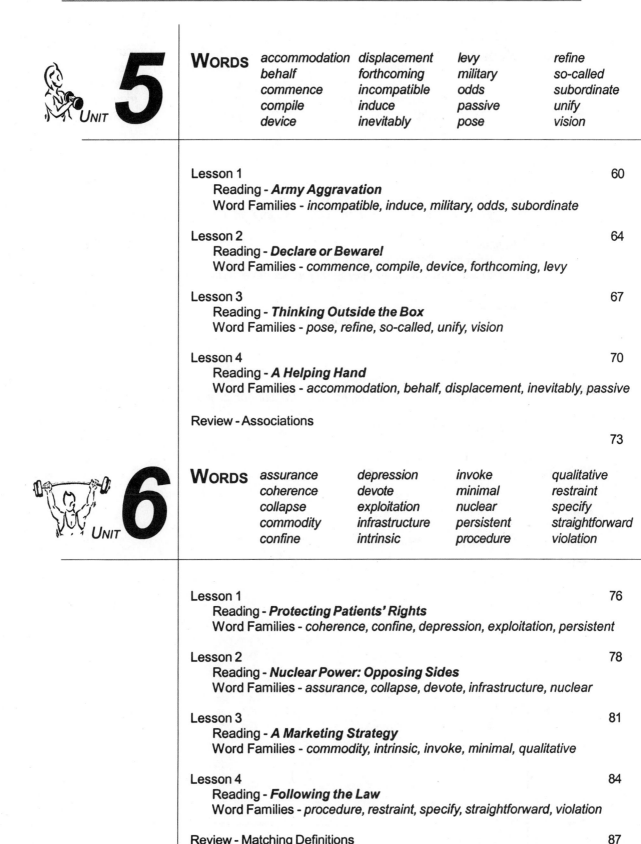

WORDS   5

accommodation	displacement	levy	refine
behalf	forthcoming	military	so-called
commence	incompatible	odds	subordinate
compile	induce	passive	unify
device	inevitably	pose	vision

WORDS   6

assurance	depression	invoke	qualitative
coherence	devote	minimal	restraint
collapse	exploitation	nuclear	specify
commodity	infrastructure	persistent	straightforward
confine	intrinsic	procedure	violation

7 UNIT

WORDS

albeit	distort	mutual	route
complement	implicit	notwithstanding	scenario
conceive	inclination	offset	suspend
concurrent	integral	practitioner	trigger
controversy	mediate	protocol	whereby

INTRODUCTION

WELCOME TO *ACADEMIC WORD POWER*!

ACADEMIC WORD POWER is a four-volume vocabulary series for students of English at the high school or college level who are planning to pursue further academic studies. The goal of the series is to help students learn the vocabulary they need for success in academic reading and writing.

ACADEMIC WORD POWER 1 is designed for intermediate students.

ACADEMIC WORD POWER 2, 3, and *4* are designed for high-intermediate, advanced, and high-advanced levels, respectively.

The target vocabulary in all four volumes was selected from the Academic Word List (AWL) developed by Averil Coxhead in 1998. The AWL, which contains 570 words, was compiled from a corpus of 3.5 million words found in academic texts. When students add the words from this list to a basic vocabulary of 2000 words, they will be able to comprehend approximately 90 percent of the vocabulary in academic texts. When proper nouns and technical vocabulary are added to this, students approach the 95 percent comprehension level that research has shown is needed for successful academic reading.

TO THE TEACHER . . .

Series Approach

Reflecting the latest research in vocabulary acquisition and pedagogy, the exercises and activities in this text are based on an interactive approach to vocabulary instruction. Consequently, the reading, writing and speaking exercises give the student multiple exposures to the target words in meaningful contexts and provide rich information about each word. The exercises also establish ties between the target words and the student's prior knowledge and experience.

About the Books

Each volume has seven units that target 20 AWL words per unit. Thus, 140 AWL words are studied in each book, and 560 of the 570 words on the AWL are covered in the four volumes. The AWL words were sequenced and grouped into the four volumes by taking into consideration the frequency of the words, their level of difficulty and the thematic relationships between the words. A great variety of vocabulary development practice activities as well as strategies for learning and remembering academic vocabulary are incorporated in each book.

Text Organization

The seven units in each book are divided into four lessons that focus on five AWL words. Every lesson includes the following components:

- **Word Families**: This section introduces the five target words by providing a head word, which is the most frequently used in academic texts, as well as other word forms of the target word. A chart is provided for students to place the different word forms under the correct part of speech. This focus on word families helps students decipher new words and build spelling proficiency.

- **Reading**: A one-paragraph reading introduces students to the five target words in an academic context.

- **Comprehension Check:** Two exercises check students' superficial comprehension of the target words. For the first exercise, students match definitions by using the context provided in the reading in the previous section. The second exercise includes exercises such as true/false statements, yes/no questions, odd man out, fill in the blank, or matching sentence halves.

- **Word Study**: This section provides rich instruction through exercises that offer an expansion of the target words. This is accomplished through a wide variety of exercises, such as collocations, multiple meanings, grammar application, word form practice, analogies, pronunciation tips, and idiomatic usage. Both the written exercises in this section and the previous section are designed to be completed quickly by students and graded easily by teachers because research shows that the type of written exercise is not significant in terms of retention. Rather, it is the number of retrievals that is significant. Thus, it is better to have a larger quantity of exercises that can be done quickly as opposed to a smaller number of exercises that are time-consuming to complete (such as writing original sentences with the target words).

- **Using Words in Communication:** Communicative activities in this section give students practice in using the target words fluently. The students use the target words orally in different settings, such as sentence completion, discussion, role-play, interviewing, summariz ing, paraphrasing, storytelling, listing ideas related to the target word, or associating the target word with other words from the unit. These activities aid in retention of the target words as they develop a link between the target words and students' past experience and knowledge.

Other features of the series include:

- **Unit Reviews:** Each unit ends with an exercise that reviews all 20 words from the unit through an easy-to-do, fun activity, such as a crossword puzzle, find-a-word, word scramble, sentence scramble, associations, and definition match-up.

- **Website:** All four volumes have a companion website with an instructor and student site. This site can be accessed at www.college.hmco.com/esl. The instructor site includes unit assessments and the answer key for the book. The student site includes longer readings with the target AWL words, vocabulary flashcards, and review quizzes for each lesson.

- **Easy to supplement with writing activities**: If a teacher wants to do more extensive writing practice with the target words, the books can be easily supplemented with writing activities such as writing original sentences, paragraphs and essays with the AWL words.

TO THE STUDENT . . .

Did you know the following facts?

- The average native English-speaking university student has a vocabulary of around 21,000 words.

- The average adult ESL student learns about 2,500 English words per year.

Before you get depressed and discouraged, consider the following fact: English (like any other language) uses a relatively small number of words over and over again. Words that are used over and over again are called "high frequency" words. The words you will be studying in this book come from a high frequency list called the *Academic Word List* (AWL). The AWL contains 570 words that frequently occur in academic texts, such as university textbooks, course workbooks, and academic journal articles.

Why is it a good use of your time and energy to learn the words on the AWL?

If you add the 570 words on the AWL list to a basic vocabulary of 2000 English words (which most intermediate readers already have), you'll be able to understand 90% of the words in an average academic text. This book will help you learn many of the words on the AWL through numerous written exercises that introduce you to the meanings of the words and provide important information about the words, such as word forms, idiomatic uses, and pronunciation tips. This book also has many speaking activities that will give you practice using the new words fluently.

Besides completing all the exercises in the book, it is recommended that you use vocabulary cards to help you remember the new words. On the next page are some tips (advice) on how to make vocabulary cards.

HOW TO MAKE YOUR OWN VOCABULARY CARDS

1. Use small cards (no bigger than 3 by 5 inch) so that they can be easily carried.

2. Put the new word on one side and the definition (meaning) on the other side.

3. In addition to the definition, you can include the following information on the back side of the card:

   - a translation of the new word in your language;
   - pictures or diagrams related to the new word;
   - phonetic pronunciation;
   - a sample sentence using the new word.

4. Practice with the cards by looking at the new word and trying to recall the meaning first, and then (later) by looking at the meaning and trying to recall the new word.

5. Say the words aloud or to yourself when you are studying the cards.

6. Study the cards frequently. When you learn a new word, try to study it later that day, the next day, the next week, and then a few weeks later.

7. Study the words with a partner occasionally. When reviewing with a partner, try to use the word in a new sentence.

8. Change the order of the cards frequently. Don't order the cards alphabetically or put the cards in groups of similar words. Words which look the same or have similar meanings are easy to confuse.

GUIDE TO PRONUNCIATION

Vowels

Symbol	Key Word	Pronunciation
/ɑ/	hot	/hɑt/
/æ/	cat	/kæt/
/aɪ/	tie	/taɪ/
/aʊ/	cow	/kaʊ/
/ɛ/	bed	/bɛd/
/eɪ/	same	/seɪm/
/i/	he	/hɪ/
/ɪ/	it	/ɪt/
/oʊ/	go	/goʊ/
/ʊ/	book	/bʊk/
/ɔ/	dog	/dɔg/
/ɔɪ/	boy	/bɔɪ/
/ʌ/	cup	/kʌp/
/ɜr/	bird	/bɜrd/
/ə/	about	/əˈbaʊt/
	softer	/ˈsɔftər/

Consonants

Symbol	Key Word	Pronunciation
/b/	be	/bi/
/d/	did	/dɪd/
/dʒ/	jump	/dʒʌmp/
/f/	fat	/fæt/
/g/	go	/goʊ/
/h/	hit	/hɪt/
/k/	cat	/kæt/
/l/	life	/laɪf/
/m/	me	/mi/
/n/	no	/noʊ/
/ŋ/	sing	/sɪŋ/
/p/	pen	/pɛn/
/r/	red	/rɛd/
/s/	see	/si/
/t/	tea	/ti/
/tʃ/	cheap	/tʃip/
/v/	vote	/voʊt/
/w/	we	/wi/
/z/	zoo	/zʊ/
/ð/	they	/ðeɪ/
/θ/	thin	/θɪn/

GUIDE TO SYLLABLE STRESS

/ˈ/   open   /ˈoʊpən/
used before a syllable to show primary stress

/ˌ/   doorway   /ˈdɔrˌweɪ/
used before a syllable to show secondary stress

ACKNOWLEDGEMENTS

Many thanks to Averil Coxhead for giving us permission to use the *Academic Word List* (AWL) in the development of this series. It is hard to imagine the hours of planning and labor that went into compiling this list from such an extensive corpus (3.5 million running words from over 400 academic texts). For more information about the AWL see the article *A New Academic Word List* by Averil Coxhead in the Summer 2000 TESOL Quarterly.

Also, thanks to Barbara Hefka, an instructor at the University of North Texas Intensive English Language Institute (IELI) for sequencing and grouping the 570 words on the AWL for the four volumes in this series. When sequencing these words, Barbara had to take in consideration the frequency of the words, their level of difficulty, and thematic relationships between the words. It was a herculean task that only someone with Barbara's breadth of ESL experience and teaching intuition could have handled so well.

Huge thanks go to Judith Kulp, a publishing coordinator at UNT, for her invaluable, professional input on this project. Thanks also go to M. J. Weaver for her production skills, and to Yun Ju Kim, a communication design student at UNT, who created the graphics for the series.

Finally, thanks to Eva Bowman, Director of the IELI, and Dr. Rebecca Smith-Murdock, Director of International Programs, for their support in the development of the series. They had faith in my vision for the series and in the writing and creative abilities of the four authors: Lisa Hollinger, Celia Thompson, Pat Bull, and Barbara Jones.

- Donna Obenda

UNIT 1

WORDS

accumulate	component	hence	relax
anticipate	conference	index	tape
bond	conversely	ministry	technical
channel	enable	overseas	visual
colleague	file	paradigm	whereas

READINGS
A Great Opportunity
Vocabulary Tips
Sharing Resources
New Car Phones

STRATEGIES AND SKILLS
Word Forms
- Word family chart
- Word form selection

Comprehension Check
- Matching definitions
- Identifying synonyms
- Understanding words in context

Word Expansion
- Grammar application
- Multiple meaning
- Collocations

Interactive Speaking Practice
- Discussion
- Listing
- Summarizing

ACADEMIC WORD POWER

LESSON 1

A. WORD FAMILIES

Study the five word families below. Then fill in the word form chart. The underlined word forms at the top of the list are the most commonly used forms in academic texts.

colleague	ministry	conversely	overseas (2X)*	bond (2X)*
/ˈkɑˌlig/	/ˈmɪnəstri/	/kənˈvɜrsli/	/ˌoʊvərˈsiz/	/bɑnd/
	ministerial	converse		bonded
	minister (2X)			bonding

* used 2 times in the word form chart

Exercise - Word Form Chart

NOUN	VERB	ADJECTIVE	ADVERB
1. colleague			
1. ministry 2. minister	1. minister	1. ministerial	
		1. converse	1. conversely
		1. overseas	1. overseas
1. bond	1. bond	1. bonded 2. bonding	

B. READING

A Great Opportunity

When Janet was hired by the Italian Ministry of Education to help with English language training courses, she was thrilled by the opportunity to go overseas and learn about a different culture. She learned the language and developed strong bonds with her Italian friends and colleagues. Conversely, her husband was terribly homesick the whole time they were in Italy and made no effort to adapt to the new culture.

C. COMPREHENSION CHECK
Exercise 1

Refer to the reading above and use the context to guess the meanings of the words below. Then match the words to their definitions. Do NOT use a dictionary.

C 1. colleagues   A. in a foreign location across an ocean

D 2. ministry   B. strong connections

E 3. conversely   C. people you work with

A 4. overseas   D. high government department

B 5. bonds   E. in a contrasting way

Exercise 2
Which word does not belong?

1.	colleague	partner	coworker	cohort	(enemy)
2.	conversely	in contrast	(meanwhile)	however	on the other hand
3.	bond	link	attachment	(disagreement)	tie

D. WORD STUDY
Exercise 1
Many words in English are commonly used with certain prepositions. Find these words (or forms of these words) in the reading and write the prepositions that go with them on the line provided. (Hint: one of the words does not have a preposition that goes with it.)

1. ministry   _of_
2. bond   _with_
3. overseas   _____

Exercise 2
Some words have more than one commonly used meaning or are easily confused with similar words. Look at the examples below and at the top of the next page.

---

1. **colleague vs. coworker** - While any people who work together at the same job can be called coworkers, colleagues are usually people working together in a similar professional position.

2. **ministry vs. department** - While official government agencies are referred to as ministries in many countries (for example, in England, the Ministry of Education), they are called departments in other countries (for example, in the United States, the Department of Education).

3. **government minister vs. religious minister** - The leader of a government ministry (such as the Ministry of Agriculture) is referred to as the Minister of Agriculture. However, the leader of some churches in the Christian religion is called the minister of the church.

4. **to minister to (religion vs. health)** - While a church minister ministers to the spiritual needs of the church members, doctors, nurses, family or friends can minister to the needs of a sick person by taking care of their physical and, perhaps, emotional needs.

5. **emotional vs. physical bond** - People or animals bond emotionally when they develop a very close feeling of connection. For example, newborn animals bond with the first animal they encounter, which is usually their mother. The word bond also refers to a physical connection that usually involves gluing or sealing two objects together.

---

good ex. of figurative & literal →

Write YES if the underlined word is used correctly and NO if it is used incorrectly.

_No_ 1. Fred invited his <u>colleague</u> from the factory assembly line to his party.

_No_ 2. The U.S. <u>Ministry</u> of Health, Education, and Welfare is located in Washington, DC.

_Y_ 3. Mrs. McConnell <u>ministered</u> to all her sick husband's needs for 20 years.

_Y_ 4. The <u>minister</u> of the Methodist Church met with other church leaders in the town to discuss ways to help poor people in the community.

_Y_ 5. Be careful with that superglue! Once two things are stuck together, it's almost impossible to break the <u>bond</u>.

_Y_ 6. <u>Coworkers</u> from all levels of the company gathered together for the 40 year anniversary celebration.

E. USING WORDS IN COMMUNICATION
Exercise

1. Describe the ideal <u>colleague</u>. Conversely, what are the characteristics of a bad <u>colleague</u>?

2. Describe three <u>overseas</u> locations you would like to visit and explain why.

3. Is it common for adult children to <u>minister</u> to the needs of their aging parents? Do you have strong <u>bonds</u> with your parents?

LESSON 2

A. WORD FAMILIES

Study the five word families below. Then fill in the word form chart. The underlined word forms at the top of the list are the most commonly used forms in academic texts.

file (2X)	relax	tape (2X)	enable	index (2X)
/faɪl/	/rə ˈlæks/	/teɪp/	/ɛn ˈeɪbəl/	/ˈɪnˌdɛks/
filed	relaxation	taped		
filing	relaxing			
	relaxed			

Exercise - Word Form Chart

NOUN	VERB	ADJECTIVE	ADVERB
1. file	1. *file*	1. *filed* 2. *filing*	
1. *relaxation*	1. relax	1. *relaxing* 2. *relaxed*	
1. tape	1. *tape*	1. *taped*	
	1. enable		
1. index	1. *index*		

B. READING

Vocabulary Tips

When you have a lot of new vocabulary words to learn, it might be a good idea to write them on <u>index</u> cards and keep them alphabetically organized in a <u>file</u>. You could also ask your teacher to pronounce them while you record her voice onto a <u>tape</u>. Most importantly, spending time reviewing the words every day will <u>enable</u> you to learn them thoroughly, and then you can <u>relax</u> when it's time for the vocabulary test!

C. COMPREHENSION CHECK
Exercise 1

Refer to the reading above and use the context to guess the meanings of the words below. Then match the words to their definitions. Do NOT use a dictionary.

A 1. index   A. alphabetical or otherwise organized list
D 2. file   B. cassette used for recording and playing sounds
B 3. tape   C. feel at ease
E 4. enable   D. receptacle for organized notes, papers, cards etc
C 5. relax   E. make possible

Exercise 2

Circle the word that does not belong.

1. enjoy	release	relax	tense
2. tape	film	display	cassette
3. limit	enable	help	allow
4. file	box	cabinet	television
5. list	itemization	pencil	index

D. WORD STUDY

Exercise

Study the three ways to use the verb **relax** and the multiple meanings of **file** and **tape**. Then do the YES/NO exercise that follows.

---

1. relax (v) - Intransitive (S + V) : *Jack works too hard. He should relax.*
   Transitive (S + V + O) : *The massage relaxed his back muscles.*
   Collocation (S + V + O + on something) : *He lost control of the car when he relaxed his grip on the wheel.*

---

2. file (n) - receptacle for organized notes etc

3. file (n) - rough edged metal instrument for smoothing a surface

4. file (n) - a line :*They entered the room in a single file.*

---

5. tape (n) - audio or video cassette

6. tape (n) - piece of adhesive material for wrapping or attaching something

---

YES or NO? Write Y or N in the blanks provided.

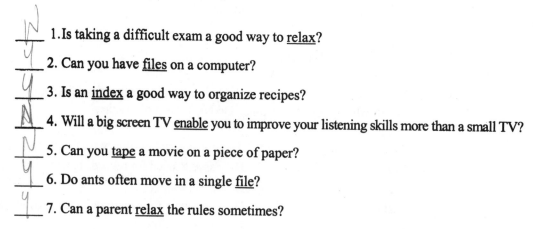

_N_ 1. Is taking a difficult exam a good way to <u>relax</u>?

_Y_ 2. Can you have <u>files</u> on a computer?

_Y_ 3. Is an <u>index</u> a good way to organize recipes?

_N_ 4. Will a big screen TV <u>enable</u> you to improve your listening skills more than a small TV?

_N_ 5. Can you <u>tape</u> a movie on a piece of paper?

_Y_ 6. Do ants often move in a single <u>file</u>?

_Y_ 7. Can a parent <u>relax</u> the rules sometimes?

6

E. USING WORDS IN COMMUNICATION
Exercise

1. List 3 ways to <u>index</u> new vocabulary words

2. List 3 video <u>tapes</u> you have watched (or 3 cassette <u>tapes</u> you've listened to) recently.

3. List 3 <u>factors</u> that have enabled you to study English.

4. List 3 good ways to <u>relax</u>.

LESSON 3

A. WORD FAMILIES

Study the five word families below. Then fill in the word form chart. The underlined word forms at the top of the list are the most commonly used forms in academic texts.

technical	visual	accumulation	hence	channel (2X)
/ˈtɛknəkəl/	/ˈvɪdʒuəl/	/əˌkyumyəˈleɪʃən/	/hɛns/	/ˈtʃænl/
technically	visualization	accumulate		channeled
	visualize	accumulated		
	visually	accumulating		

Exercise - Word Form Chart

NOUN	VERB	ADJECTIVE	ADVERB
		1. technical	1.
1.	1.	1. visual 2.	1.
1. accumulation	1.	1. 2.	
			1. hence
1.	1. channel	1.	

B. READING

Sharing Resources

When Dr. Hill retired and started cleaning out his office, he discovered a large <u>accumulation</u> of pictures, charts and maps that he no longer needed. With some <u>technical</u> assistance from the computer lab director, he was able to scan these <u>visual</u> aids and <u>channel</u> them to other teachers over the internet. <u>Hence</u>, classes all over the country were able to benefit from his accumulated resource material.

C. COMPREHENSION CHECK
Exercise 1

Refer to the reading above and use the context to guess the meanings of the words below. Then match the words to their definitions. Do NOT use a dictionary.

____ 1. channel   A. involving sight
____ 2. visual   B. related to a systematic, specialized procedure
____ 3. hence   C. collection, amassed gathering
____ 4. accumulation   D. direct along a specific route of communication
____ 5. technical   E. for this reason

Exercise 2
Circle the word that does not belong.

1. channel   shorten   direct   conduct
2. however   so   hence   therefore
3. sensory   visual   visible   valuable
4. discount   mass   collection   accumulation
5. systematic   poetic   technical   specialized

D. WORD STUDY
Exercise 1
Study the multiple meanings of the words **channel** and **hence**.

---

1. channel (n) - a pathway of communication

2. channel (n) - the place on the TV dial for a TV station

3. channel (n) - a waterway

---

4. hence (adv) - If "hence" means "thus", it is preceded by a semicolon and
    followed by a comma. (*He didn't study; hence, he failed.*)

5. hence (adv) - If "hence" means "from now on", no punctuation is added.
    (*Three days hence we leave.*) This is a very formal usage.

True or False? Write T or F in the blanks provided.

____ 1. E-mail is a very convenient <u>channel</u> for communicating with large groups of
people.

____ 2. Venice, Italy, has many <u>channels</u> that are used like streets throughout the city.

____ 3. She ate too much; <u>hence</u>, she is hungry.

____ 4. A truck can travel through a <u>channel</u>.

____ 5. John had his tenth birthday today. He was born ten years <u>hence</u>.

____ 6. You can use a remote control to change the television <u>channel</u>.

Exercise 2
Choose the correct word form for each blank.

1. Advertisers try to reach potential customers through a variety of _____ ,
   such as TV commercials, newspaper ads, and phone calls.
   a. channeling   b. channel   c. channeled   d. channels

2. On his tax form, John's _____ wealth was totaled at $5,797,450,000.
   a. accumulated   b. accumulation   c. accumulate   d. accumulating

3. Bright colors and moving objects are good additions to a baby's room because they
   are _____ stimulating.
   a. visual   b. visualize   c. visually   d. visualization

E. USING WORDS IN COMMUNICATION
Exercise
With a partner, discuss the following questions.

1. Can you <u>visualize</u> your life 10 years from now? What do you see? Do you like what
   you see, or do you want to change it?

2. Do you get rid of things easily or do you tend to <u>accumulate</u> a lot of things? What
   kind of things have you <u>accumulated</u> as a student? How long do you think you will
   keep them?

3. Which <u>visual</u> aids are most helpful to you in your studies? Why?

LESSON 4

A. WORD FAMILIES

Study the five word families below. Then fill in the word form chart. The underlined word forms at the top of the list are the most commonly used forms in academic texts.

component	paradigm	anticipate	whereas	conference
/kəm ˈpounənt/	/ˈpærə͵daɪm/	/æn ˈtɪsə͵peɪt/	/wɛr ˈæz/	/ˈkɑnfrəs/
		anticipation		confer
		anticipated		
		unanticipated		

Exercise - Word Form Chart

NOUN	VERB	ADJECTIVE	CONJUNCTION
1. component			
1. paradigm			
1.	1. anticipate	1. 2.	
			1. whereas
1. conference	1.		

B. READING

New Car Phones

The delegates entering the <u>conference</u> hall eagerly <u>anticipated</u> the demonstration of the recently developed voice control for car phones. This new <u>component</u> was expected to become the <u>paradigm</u> for safe car phones of the future, <u>whereas</u> the older hand held phones were expected to disappear from the market.

C. COMPREHENSION CHECK
Exercise 1
Refer to the reading above and use the context to guess the meanings of the words below. Then match the words to their definitions. Do NOT use a dictionary.

____ 1. component   A. expected, envisioned

____ 2. paradigm   B. by contrast

____ 3. anticipated   C. a part of a whole

____ 4. whereas   D. professional meeting, convention

____ 5. conference   E. model used as standard for evaluation

Exercise 2

Write YES if the underlined word is used correctly or NO if the word is used incorrectly.

_____1. An ant hill could be seen as a <u>paradigm</u> for a community effort.

_____2. Boston is on the east coast, <u>whereas</u> New York is also in the eastern U.S.

_____3. The purpose of a <u>conference</u> is to share ideas and information.

_____4. Hondas and Chevrolets are <u>components</u> of cars.

_____5. If you turn your lecture notes into questions, you can <u>anticipate</u> what will be asked on the test.

D. WORD STUDY

Exercise 1

In the English language, certain words are used together regularly and sound correct together. These are called collocations. For example, a common collocation with <u>paradigm</u>, one of the words from this unit 1, is <u>paradigm for how</u>. Another example of a collocation with a word from this lesson is <u>in anticipation of</u>. Study the explanations and then do the exercise that follows.

---

1. paradigm - (something) is a paradigm for how + S + V (+ O)

   Example: The brain is a paradigm for how a computer works.

---

2. anticipation - (do something) in anticipation of (something)

   Example: He closed the windows in anticipation of the storm.

Write YES is the underlined phrase is used correctly or NO if the phrase is used incorrectly.

_____1. The Romano family moved to a smaller apartment <u>in anticipation of</u> winning the lottery.

_____2. Madonna is <u>a paradigm for</u> how a person can become a successful musician.

_____3. Kathy baked a cake <u>in anticipation of</u> her roommate's birthday party.

_____4. Using a fork to eat is <u>a paradigm for</u> using a knife to cut food.

E. USING WORDS IN COMMUNICATION

Exercise 1

Reread the reading at the beginning of this lesson. Then close your book. Without looking at the reading, give your partner a summary of the reading using as many of the vocabulary words as you can.

Exercise 2

With a partner, discuss the following:

1. Describe the most important <u>components</u> of a good language program.

2. What are some activities that you <u>anticipate</u> doing in the coming week?

3. What will you do in <u>anticipation</u> of your next vacation?

REVIEW

Use words from the list at the beginning of this unit to fill in the blanks.
Then add the words to the puzzle on the following page.

ACROSS

2. Class is over, so we can put our books aside and _relax_ .
5. Jackie Kennedy was seen as a _paradigm_ for how a First Lady should behave.
6. Sergeant Cooke was able to _tape_ the entire conversation with the drug dealer on his hidden recorder.
7. For a computer problem, ask the lab director for _technical_ assistance.
11. To meet with the CEO, you have to go through the appropriate _channels_ .
12. Leaders from all over the world attended the _conference_ on global warming.
17. Exercise speeds up your metabolism; _conversely_ , laziness slows it down.
18. _Visual_ learners like to see the information they are learning. Just hearing it is not as helpful for them.
19. The _bonds_ of marriage were much harder to break 100 years ago.
20. Vocabulary building is an essential _component_ of a good language program.

DOWN

1. It's hard to _anticipate_ how expensive it can be to raise children before you actually have   children of your own.
3. Winning a full scholarship will _enable_ Sarah to attend the university of her choice next year.
4. It's good to make a separate computer _file_ for each of your classes so that the   information is easy to find.
8. No one could pronounce his name; _hence_ he changed it to John.
9. Peter and another _colleague_ worked together to design the new shopping center.
10. Representatives from the _ministry_ of Health met in London.
13. Brad is excited about his upcoming trip to Africa. He's never been _overseas_ .
14. A heavy _accumulation_ of snow on the old roof finally caused it to collapse.
15. Paris, France is famous to people around the world, _whereas_ Paris, Texas is relatively unknown.
16. Check the _index_ in the back of the book to find more information about the topic.

UNIT 2

WORDS

assemble	corporate	grade	panel
attain	denote	implication	plus
chemical	duration	integrity	regime
code	entity	likewise	sphere
contrary	federal	mechanism	team

READINGS

Safety First
Plagiarism Doesn't Pay
Climbing the Corporate Ladder
National Strength

STRATEGIES AND SKILLS

Word Forms
- Word family chart
- Word form selection

Comprehension Check
- Matching definitions
- Using words in context
- Identifying synonyms

Word Expansion
- Multiple meaning
- Collocations
- Connotation

Interactive Speaking Practice
- Summarizing
- Listing
- Discussion

ACADEMIC WORD POWER

LESSON 1

A. WORD FAMILIES

Study the five word families below. Then fill in the word form chart. The underlined word forms at the top of the list are the most commonly used forms in academic texts.

chemical (2X)	assembly	mechanism	entity	likewise
/'kɛmɪkəl/	/ə'sɛmbli/	/mɛkə,nɪzəm/	/'ɛntəti/	/'laɪk,waɪz/
chemically	assembled			
	assemble			

Exercise - Word Form Chart

NOUN	VERB	ADJECTIVE	ADVERB
1.		1. chemical	1.
1. assembly	1.	1.	
1. mechanism			
1. entity			
			1. likewise

B. READING

Safety First

A nuclear power plants is usually set up as a self-contained <u>entity</u>. Its <u>assembly</u> includes built-in safeguards in order to prevent any problem, such as leakage, from growing into a greater catastrophe. <u>Likewise</u>, a <u>chemical</u> plant is required to have safety <u>mechanisms</u> in place to deal with fires or explosions.

C. COMPREHENSION CHECK
Exercise 1
Refer to the reading above and use the context to guess the meanings of the words below. Then match the words to their definitions. Do NOT use a dictionary.

____ 1. chemical   A. a group viewed as a whole

____ 2. assembly   B. parts of a machine that move to do something

____ 3. mechanisms   C. having to do with the science of matter

____ 4. entity   D. in addition, in the same way or manner

____ 5. likewise   E. putting parts of something together

Exercise 2
Write one word from Exercise 1 in each of the blanks.

1. Potassium Sulfate is a _____ combination.

2. In the United States, the church is a separate _____ from the state.

3. A clock has a small _____ that you can turn to change the time.

4. The _____ of the bookcase took us five hours!

5. The moon revolves around Earth; _____ , Earth revolves around the sun.

D. WORD STUDY
Exercise
Some words have more than one commonly used meaning or are easily confused with similar words. Look at the examples below.

---

1. assemble (v) - to put things together

2. assembly (n) - grouping or gathering of people

---

3. mechanism (n) - part of a machine

4. mechanism (n) - means of doing something

Write YES if the underlined word is used correctly and NO if it is used incorrectly.

_____ 1. The United Nations General <u>Assembly</u> passes resolutions regarding global issues.

_____ 2. In order to <u>assemble</u> a bicycle, you should take off the wheels, and then remove the pedals.

_____ 3. Repression is a defense <u>mechanism</u> used by the brain to ignore an unwanted idea or thought.

_____ 4. Most people agree that all countries should <u>assemble</u> more nuclear bombs.

_____ 5. This computer program has a <u>mechanism</u> for checking spelling.

_____ 6. The principal of the school announced to the student <u>assembly</u> that scholarships had been awarded to several members of the senior class.

_____ 7. The cocktail party was organized as a <u>mechanism</u> for the new employees to meet their future colleagues in an informal setting.

E. USING WORDS IN COMMUNICATION
Exercise

Reread the reading at the beginning of this lesson. Then close your book. Without looking at the reading, give your partner a summary of the reading using as many of the vocabulary words as you can.

LESSON 2

A. WORD FAMILIES

Study the five word families below. Then fill in the word form chart. The underlined word forms at the top of the list are the most commonly used forms in academic texts.

contrary	grade (2X)	code (2X)	integrity	panel (2X)
/kɑn ˌtrɛri/	/greɪd/	/koʊd/	/ɪn ˈtɛgrəti/	/ˈpænəl/
contrarily	graded	coded		paneled

Exercise - Word Form Chart

NOUN	VERB	ADJECTIVE	ADVERB
		1. contrary	1.
1. grade	1.	1.	
1. code	1.	1.	
1. integrity			
1. panel	1.	1.	

B. READING

Plagiarism Doesn't Pay

The <u>panel</u> of professors who reviewed the charges of plagiarism against the student agreed that she had broken a <u>code</u> of appropriate behavior and had also shown a further lack of <u>integrity</u> by continuing to say it was her own work when her teacher confronted her. The teacher could easily see that the polished writing style was <u>contrary</u> to anything she had written before, and he soon found the sources she had copied. The panel decided to give her a failing <u>grade</u> for the course and suspend her for one semester.

C. COMPREHENSION CHECK
Exercise 1

Refer to the reading above and use the context to guess the meanings of the words below. Then match the words to their definitions. Do NOT use a dictionary.

___ 1. contrary	A. academic score
___ 2. grade	B. strong morals, honesty
___ 3. code	C. group of people chosen to discuss issues
___ 4. integrity	D. different from, opposite
___ 5. panel	E. set of rules for behavior

Exercise 2
Circle the word that does not belong.

1. opposite	contrary	different	similar
2. panel	group	individual	committee
3. book	mark	score	grade
4. rules	code	guideline	jacket
5. integrity	tricks	honesty	morals

D. WORD STUDY
Exercise
Some words have more than one commonly used meaning. Look at the examples below.

```
1.  panel (n) - group that discusses and/or makes decisions
2.  panel (n) - distinct part of a surface, such as a wall
3.  panel (n) - surface with buttons, dials, controls
```

```
4.  code (n) - secret formula
5.  code (n) - set of rules
```

```
6.  grade (n) - score
7.  grade (n) - academic level
8.  grade (n) - level of quality
9.  grade (n) - degree of incline
```

```
10. integrity (n) - honesty, high moral values
11. integrity (n) - strength, completeness
```

```
12. contrary (adj) - opposite
13. contrary (adj) - uncooperative, difficult to work with
```

Write YES if the sentence uses the vocabulary word correctly, or NO if it does not.

_____ 1. His angry reaction was <u>contrary</u> to what we had expected.

_____ 2. The police arrested Leslie because of her <u>integrity</u>.

_____ 3. He sent a <u>coded</u> message so everyone could understand it easily.

_____ 4. The <u>integrity</u> of the structure was compromised by the earthquake.

_____ 5. I like to sprinkle <u>graded</u> cheese on my salad.

_____ 6. The dress <u>code</u> has been modified; now it's okay to wear blue jeans.

_____ 7. I prefer <u>Grade</u> A butter.

_____ 8. The instrument <u>panel</u> was so clearly marked that even a child could fly the plane.

_____ 9. The <u>integrity</u> of the team comes from working well together.

_____ 10. Martha was such a <u>contrary</u> person that she was chosen to lead the panel discussion.

E. USING WORDS IN COMMUNICATION
Exercise

1. List 3 things that are <u>contrary</u> to what you expected to experience as a high school or university student.

2. List 3 things that you would include in a <u>code</u> of behavior for an elementary school.

LESSON 3

A. WORD FAMILIES

Study the five word families below. Then fill in the word form chart. The underlined word forms at the top of the list are the most commonly used forms in academic texts.

corporate	attain	sphere	team (2X)	plus (2X)
/ˈkɔrprɪt/	/ə ˈteɪn/	/sfɪr/	/tim/	/plʌs/
corporation	(un)attainable	spherical		
	(un)attained			

Exercise - Word Form Chart

NOUN	VERB	ADJECTIVE	PREPOSITION
1.		1. corporate	
	1. attain	1. 2.	
1. sphere		1.	
1. team	1.		
1. plus			1.

B. READING

Climbing the Corporate Ladder

If you want to <u>attain</u> a high position in the <u>corporate</u> world, you should first demonstrate your ability to work well on a <u>team</u>. Then, in order to rise to the executive <u>sphere</u>, you need to display your leadership abilities. Of course, being in the right place at the right time is also a <u>plus</u>!

C. COMPREHENSION CHECK
Exercise 1

Refer to the reading above and use the context to guess the meanings of the words below. Then match the words to their definitions. Do NOT use a dictionary.

_b_ 1. corporate   A. an area, circle of influence

_e_ 2. attain   B. related to a large business

_a_ 3. sphere   C. bonus, good addition

_d_ 4. team   D. two or more people/animals working together

_c_ 5. plus   E. reach, achieve

Exercise 2
Which word does not belong?

1. group   pair   team   individual
2. sphere   square   world   arena
3. obtain   attain   lose   reach
4. benefit   addition   total   plus
5. corporate   business   physical   entrepreneurial

D. WORD STUDY
Exercise
These are some common collocations for words in this unit.

corporate world	sphere of influence	to team up with someone
corporate structure		

Circle the letter of the correct answer for these collocations.

1. Which of the following would not be an important part of the corporate world?
    a. business meetings
    b. labor disputes
    c. holiday parades

2. What would be part of a corporate structure?
    a. entryways
    b. entry level positions
    c. entertainers

3. Which of these is not a sphere of influence?
    a. an employer's employees
    b. a mayor's supporters
    c. a soldier's enemies

4. In which situation would it not be a good idea to team up with someone?
    a. during a final exam
    b. during a dance contest
    c. during double tennis match

E. USING WORDS IN COMMUNICATION
Exercise
Discuss these questions with your partner.

1. Do you prefer <u>team</u> or individual sports and activities? Why?

2. When you are on a <u>team</u>, do you prefer to be a leader or a follower?
    Is it better for a <u>team</u> to have a leader or to have all the members share
    responsibility equally?

3. What are your goals for the next year, and how do you plan to <u>attain</u> them?

LESSON 4

A. WORD FAMILIES
Study the five word families below. Then fill in the word form chart. The underlined word forms at the top of the list are the most commonly used forms in academic texts.

federal	denote	regime	duration	implication
/ˈfɛdərəl/	/dɪ ˈnoʊt/	/reɪ ˈʒim/	/dʊ ˈreɪʃən/	/ɪmplə ˈkeɪʃən/
federation	denotation			implicate

Exercise - Word Form Chart

NOUN	VERB	ADJECTIVE	ADVERB
1.		1. federal	
1.	1. denote	*denotative*	
1. regime			
1. duration			
1. implication	1.		

B. READING

National Strength

When a government is described as a <u>federal</u> government, it <u>denotes</u> a central government that may have several smaller governing units, such as states, included in its authority. While the individual states have their own governments, the federal <u>regime</u> has the stronger power. If there is any <u>implication</u> of corruption in a state's legal system, the federal court system can step in and retry a case. A federal judge will preside for the <u>duration</u> of the new trial.

C. COMPREHENSION CHECK
Exercise 1
Refer to the reading above and use the context to guess the meanings of the words below. Then match the words to their definitions. Do NOT use a dictionary.

C 1. federal   A. to show clearly, signify

A 2. denote   B. the time that something continues to exist

D 3. regime   C. related to national government

B 4. duration   D. the government, system of ruling

E 5. implication   E. indication of criminal participation of others.

or imply, but imply & implicate are different

Exercise 2
Use each vocabulary word from Exercise 1 to fill in the blanks.

1. Congress is a branch of the ___federal___ government.

2. Because of the storm, we had to keep our seatbelts on for the ___duration___ of the flight.

3. The totalitarian ___regime___ was overthrown by the people's revolution.

4. The witness made a clear ___implication___ of wrongdoing on the part of the driver of the second car.

5. The red, orange and yellow leaves on the tree ___denote___ the arrival of autumn.

D. WORD STUDY

> **Denotation versus Connotation** - While the denotation of a word is the basic definition that can be found in a dictionary, the connotation of the same word deals with the meaning(s) that a word can have beyond its basic one.
>
> For example: The word **regime** has the basic definition (denotation) of "system of ruling, government". However, the usual connotation of the word **regime** is more negative than positive or neutral. We often refer to a dictatorship or other authoritarian government as a regime, but it is much less common to use the term regime in reference to a more open system of government.

E. USING WORDS IN COMMUNICATION

Exercise 1
Reread the reading at the beginning of this lesson. Then close your book. Without looking at the reading, give your partner a summary of the reading using as many of the vocabulary words as you can.

Exercise 2
With a partner, discuss the following:

1. Think of some common synonyms that may have different <u>connotations</u>. For example, do the words "thin", "slender", and "scrawny" have the exact same feeling attached to their meaning?

2. What would you do if you were <u>implicated</u> in a crime? Imagine a situation and make a step by step plan to prove your innocence.

REVIEW

Choose the correct vocabulary word to fit the context of the sentence.
Write the letter of your choice in the blank before the sentence.

_b_ 1. Jack saved a lot of money by buying a desk in pieces that he had to _____ at home.
   a. attain   b. assemble   c. denote

_a_ 2. If you want to enter the clubhouse, you need to know the secret _____ . It's 7-2-3-9-4.
   Don't tell anyone!
   a. code   b. panel   c. entity

_c_ 3. When you rent a video, you can find the _____ of the movie marked on the box. It's
   usually about 2 hours.
   a. mechanism   b. sphere   c. duration

_a_ 4. I resent your _____ that my sister is lazy. In fact, she works very hard!
   a. implication   b. integrity   c. regime

_c_ 5. Amy was chosen to participate in a _____ discussion with three other scientists at the
   physics conference.
   a. contrary   b. federal   c. panel

_a_ 6. If we all work as a _____ , we will finish this puzzle more quickly than if we each work alone.
   a. team   b. grade   c. corporation

_c_ 7. His _____ of influence included all the top officials in the city government.
   a. assemble   b. duration   c. sphere

_a_ 8. The new _____ replaced the recently elected government by force.
   a. regime   b. mechanism   c. implication

_c_ 9. You can _____ your goal of graduating in four years if you continue to study hard.
   a. denote   b. code   c. attain

_b_ 10. _____ to popular beliefs, colds are not caused by cold or wet weather.
   a. Likewise   b. Contrary   c. Plus

_C_ 11. The ESL program is a separate _____ from the Foreign Language Department.
  a. assembly   b. panel   c. entity

_b_ 12. _____ is one of the most important qualities in a mate. It must be terrible to live with someone who lies and can't be trusted.
  a. Federation   b. Integrity   c. Denotation

_a_ 13. Low mileage _____ a new engine make this used car a good buy.
  a. plus   b. teamed   c. paneled

_c_ 14. Smoke detectors have a special _____ that senses the presence of smoke and causes the alarm to go off.
  a. code   b. chemical   c. mechanism

_c_ 15. Canada was once an English colony; _____ , Australia used to be controlled by England.
  a. contrarily   b. implicating   c. likewise

_b_ 16. Your high _____ on the test indicates that you understand the material very well.
  a. duration   b. grade   c. sphere

_a_ 17. In the United States, there is a _____ government, but each state also has its own government.
  a. federal   b. team   c. corporate

_c_ 18. "Dr." in front of a name _____ a medical degree or a doctorate degree in some other field.
  a. attains   b. implicates   c. denotes

_c_ 19. A CEO is the highest ranking _____ executive.
  a. integrity   b. assembled   c. corporate

_b_ 20. If you mix these two substances together, you will see an interesting _____ reaction.
  a. paneled   b. chemical   c. unattainable

UNIT 3

WORDS

appendix	compound	ethical	medium
arbitrary	contact	facilitate	ongoing
bulk	diminish	founded	portion
chart	encounter	insight	reluctant
classical	expansion	mature	temporary

READINGS

Time for Beethoven
Money Management
An Ounce of Prevention
Mistakes in the New World

STRATEGIES AND SKILLS

Word Forms
  □ Word family chart
  □ Word form selection
Comprehension Check
  □ Matching definitions
  □ Identifying synonyms
  □ Understanding words in context
Word Expansion
  □ Multiple meaning
  □ Collocations
  □ Figurative usage
Interactive Speaking Practice
  □ Listing
  □ Discussion

ACADEMIC WORD POWER

LESSON 1

A. WORD FAMILIES

Study the five word families below. Then fill in the word form chart. The underlined word forms at the top of the list are the most commonly used forms in academic texts.

appendix	bulk	classical	contact (2X)	facilitate
/ə'pɛndɪks/	/bʌlk/	/'klæsɪkəl/	/'kɑn.tækt/	/fə'sɪlə.teɪt/
append	bulky	classic (2X)	contactable	facilitation
appended		classics		facilitator
				facility

Exercise - Word Form Chart

NOUN	VERB	ADJECTIVE	ADVERB
1. appendix	1.	1.	
1. bulk		1. *bulky*	
1. *Classic* 2. *classics*		1. classical 2. *classic*	
1. *contact*	1. contact	1. *contactable*	
1. *facilitation* 2. *facilitator* 3. *facility*	1. facilitate		

B. READING

Time for Beethoven

Dr. Clark, the Music History professor, only had time to briefly touch on Beethoven's major contributions to <u>classical</u> music during the lecture. She told the students that they would have to do their own research to find out about the rest of his works before the exam. Fortunately, the <u>bulk</u> of the information could be found in their textbook, and she recommended that they look in the book's <u>appendix</u> for further references to <u>facilitate</u> their work. She also added that students could <u>contact</u> her by e-mail if they had any questions.

C. COMPREHENSION CHECK
Exercise 1
Refer to the reading above and use the context to guess the meanings of the words below. Then match the words to their definitions. Do NOT use a dictionary.

_B_ 1. classical   A. make easier

_C_ 2. bulk   B. related to 18th century music

_E_ 3. appendix   C. the most of something, the majority

_A_ 4. facilitate   D. to get in touch with

_D_ 5. contact   E. something added to the end of a book

Exercise 2

True or False? Write T or F in the blanks provided.

T 1. An <u>appendix</u> often has an alphabetical list of topics.

F 2. When you eat a salad with a cup of dressing on it, the <u>bulk</u> of the calories is in the tomatoes.

T 3. If you have an emergency and need to <u>contact</u> the police, dial 911.

F 4. Michael Jackson is a <u>classical</u> musician.

T 5. Hiring a tour guide can <u>facilitate</u> your visit to a foreign city.

D. WORD STUDY

Exercise

Study the multiple uses and meanings for the following vocabulary words.

1. appendix (n) - an informative addition to the back of a book
2. appendix (n) - a small body part located on the right side of the abdomen

3. bulk (n) - the bulk of something = the biggest part of something
4. bulk (n) - nutritional bulk = indigestible fibrous residue of food in the intestine
5. bulk (n) - sold in bulk = not packaged separately or divided into units for sale
6. bulky (adj) - thick or large and difficult to handle

7. classic (n/adj) - the best example of something, something that has been important for a long time
8. classics (n, always plural) - literature of ancient Greece/Rome
9. classical (adj) - classical music = music of 18th century Europe classical art, literature etc.= coming from ancient Greece/Rome classical method = proven and accepted way

10. contact (n) - a person you can get in touch with for help
11. contact (n) - a contact lens, a small plastic disk placed on the eyeball to improve vision

12. facility (n) - ease or expertise in doing something
13. facility (n) - service(s), including the physical area(s), provided by an organization

Write YES if the underlined word is used correctly or NO if the word is used incorrectly.

Y 1. Rice sold in <u>bulk</u> is often cheaper than the same amount in a package.

N 2. Many people like the <u>classical</u> literature of the 1700's in England.

N 3. Allison is always afraid to go to parties because she has such <u>facility</u> with social situations.

Y 4. Everyone had to get down on the floor and search for Jill's lost <u>contact</u>.

Y 5. Mark was rushed to the hospital to have his appendix removed when it became clear he had appendicitis.

Y 6. The <u>facilities</u> in the new recreation center are wonderful.

E. USING WORDS IN COMMUNICATION
Exercise

1. List 3 things with which you have a <u>facility</u>.

2. List 3 <u>facilities</u> that a school should have.

3. List 3 things that are often sold in <u>bulk</u>.

4. List 3 things that you consider to be <u>classic</u>.

5. List 3 things that are <u>bulky</u>.

LESSON 2

A. WORD FAMILIES

Study the five word families below. Then fill in the word form chart. The underlined word forms at the top of the list are the most commonly used forms in academic texts.

compound (2X)	diminish	mature (2X)	medium (2X)	portion
/ˈkɑmˌpaʊnd/	/dəˈmɪnɪʃ/	/məˈtʃʊr/	/ˈmidiəm/	/ˈpɔrʃən/
compounded	diminished	maturation		
compounding	diminishing	maturational		
	diminution	matured		
	undiminished	maturity		
		immature		
		immaturity		

Exercise - Word Form Chart

NOUN	VERB	ADJECTIVE	ADVERB
1. Compound	1. compound	1. compounded 2. compounding	
1. diminution	1. diminish	1. diminished 2. diminishing 3. undiminished	
1. maturation 2. maturity 3. immaturity	1. mature	1. mature 2. maturational 3. matured 4. immature	
1. medium		1. medium	
1. portion	portion		

B. READING

Money Management

When Jason turned 25 last month, his grandmother decided he was mature enough to manage some money and gave him $20,000 to invest. He used a <u>portion</u> of the money to purchase a variety of <u>medium</u> priced stocks that were high yield but also high risk. To balance this, he also put some money into mutual funds that he hoped would provide some slower but more stable growth in case the returns on his stocks <u>diminished</u> unexpectedly. In addition, he bought some savings bonds that would <u>mature</u> about the time his daughter would be ready to go to university. He put the remainder of the money into a regular savings account that would <u>compound</u> daily and be readily accessible.

C. COMPREHENSION CHECK
Exercise 1
Refer to the preceding reading and use the context to guess the meanings of the words below. Then match the words to their definitions. Do NOT use a dictionary.

B 1. diminished   A. part of a whole

A 2. portion   B. decreased

E 3. medium   C. add on top of something else

D 4. mature   D. become ready to be collected

C 5. compound   E. in the middle range

Exercise 2
Circle the word that does not belong.

1.	whole	piece	section	portion
2.	reduced	climbed	decreased	diminished
3.	medium	middle	average	most
4.	ripe	mature	childish	grown
5.	accumulate	divide	compound	add

D. WORD STUDY
Exercise
Study the multiple meanings and uses of the vocabulary words.

1. compound (n) - something made by combining two or more parts or elements
2. compound (n) - an area with a fence around it
3. compound (v) - to make more difficult, to complicate
4. compound (v) - to add something on top of something else

5. mature physically (v) - when a living thing is fully grown with all its physical parts fully developed
6. mature emotionally (v) - when a person has developed a clear sense of responsibility and is capable of doing what is right
7. mature financially (v) - ready to be collected or due

8. medium (adj) - average sized, between large and small
9. medium (n) - a means of doing something
10. medium (n) - an environment in which something develops
11. medium (n) - a person who claims to be able to speak with spirits

Write YES if the underlined word is used correctly or NO if it is used incorrectly.

_Y_ 1. Art is a good <u>medium</u> for expressing feelings.

_N_ 2. Although Tom was only 13 years old, he was so <u>immature</u> that they let him play on the adult baseball team.

_Y_ 3. The fact that Mario didn't speak much English and his new wife didn't speak much Italian <u>compounded</u> the problems facing the newlyweds.

_Y_ 4. CO_2 is a chemical <u>compound</u> made up of one part carbon and two parts oxygen.

_N_ 5. The <u>medium</u> charged Mrs. Collins fifty dollars for a painting of her son.

_Y_ 6. The ice storm didn't hurt the <u>mature</u> trees, but some new ones fell over.

_Y_ 7. The soldiers had to have special permission to leave the <u>compound</u>.

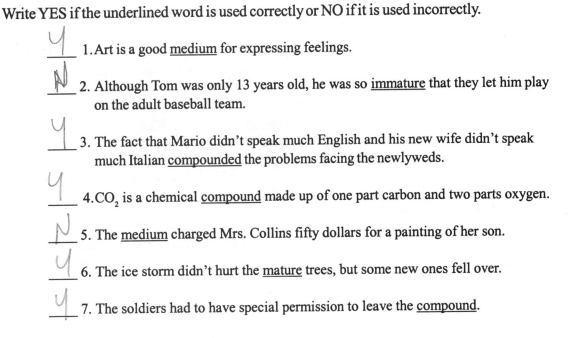

E. USING WORDS IN COMMUNICATION
Exercise
Discuss the following topics in small groups.

1. At what age is a person considered <u>mature</u> enough to be treated as an adult? Is the legal age the same as the culturally identified age?

2. At what age do you think a person is <u>mature</u> enough to vote / to drink alcohol / to serve in the army / to get married / to have children?

3. Do you know anyone who is physically <u>mature</u> yet emotionally <u>immature</u>? How about someone who is emotionally <u>mature</u> but not physically <u>mature</u>?

4. In some cultures, an extended family lives in a <u>compound</u> consisting of several buildings. In some other situations, military or company housing is located together in an area separated from the surrounding community. Would you like this kind of living arrangement? Why or why not?

5. How do you divide your monthly income or allowance? What <u>portion</u> goes to living expenses (rent, food, bills) ? What <u>portion</u> do you spend on entertainment? What <u>portion</u> do you save? Can you think of any ways to <u>compound</u> your savings?

6. What problems have <u>diminished</u> for you in the last six months? Why have they become less problematic?

LESSON 3

A. WORD FAMILIES

Study the five word families below. Then fill in the word form chart. The underlined word forms at the top of the list are the most commonly used forms in academic texts.

arbitrary	insight	ongoing	reluctant	temporary
/'arbə,treri/	/'ɪn,saɪt/	/'an,goʊɪŋ/	/rɪ 'lʌktənt/	/'tɛmpə,rɛri/
arbitrariness	insightful		reluctance	temporarily
arbitrarily			reluctantly	

Exercise - Word Form Chart

NOUN	VERB	ADJECTIVE	ADVERB
1. *arbitrariness*		1. arbitrary	1. *arbitarily*
1. insight		1. *insightful*	
		1. ongoing	
1. *reluctance*		1. reluctant	1. *reluctantly*
		1. temporary	1. *temporarily*

B. READING

An Ounce of Prevention...

AIDS research began in the 1980's, but a cure for this fatal condition has not yet been found. Scientists have gained greater <u>insights</u> into the causes of AIDS and have developed some treatments that provide <u>temporary</u> relief from the symptoms, but the search for a cure is <u>ongoing</u>. It seems that many factors associated with AIDS are quite <u>arbitrary</u> in nature. For example, some people who are sexually involved with AIDS infected partners never contract AIDS, while others become infected from a single contact. Doctors are <u>reluctant</u> to hold out too much hope for a quick solution and instead urge people to do everything possible to prevent the spread of AIDS.

C. COMPREHENSION CHECK

Exercise 1

Refer to the reading above and use the context to guess the meanings of the words below. Then match the words to their definitions. Do NOT use a dictionary.

D 1. insights   A. passing, not permanent

A 2. temporary   B. continuing

B 3. ongoing   C. coming about seemingly at random

C 4. arbitrary   D. ability to see or know the truth, *understanding*

E 5. reluctant   E. concerned or afraid, hesitant

Exercise 2
Write YES if the underlined word is used correctly or NO if it is used incorrectly.

Yes 1. A shopper can make an <u>arbitrary</u> selection at the grocery store.

No 2. An <u>ongoing</u> criminal investigation is finished.

No 3. Most people are <u>reluctant</u> to get a pay raise at work.

Yes 4. Bad weather is usually <u>temporary.</u>

Yes 5. You can gain <u>insights</u> into a country's culture by visiting that country.

D. WORD STUDY
Exercise
Many words in English are commonly used with certain prepositions or other words. Study these common collocations and then write your own sentences using them.

to gain **insight** into something	to make an **arbitrary** decision/choice
to be **reluctant** to do something	an **ongoing** investigation

1. _____.

2. _____.

3. _____.

4. _____.

E. USING WORDS IN COMMUNICATION
Exercise
Work with a partner to share information.

1. Describe a television show (or book) (or experience) that has helped you gain <u>insight</u> into something you didn't understand well before.

2. Has an authority figure (parent, teacher, boss etc) ever made an <u>arbitrary</u> decision that affected you badly? How did you feel? What did you do?

3. Describe some things that you are <u>reluctant</u> to do. Why do you hesitate to do these things? Do you want to get over your <u>reluctance</u>?

LESSON 4

A. WORD FAMILIES

Study the five word families below. Then fill in the word form chart. The underlined word forms at the top of the list are the most commonly used forms in academic texts.

chart (2X)	encounter (2X)	ethical	expansion	found
/tʃɑrt/	/ɛnˈkaʊntər/	/ˈɛθɪkəl/	/ɪkˈspænʃən/	/ˈfaʊnd/
charted		ethics	expanded	founded
uncharted		ethically	expanding	founder
		unethical	expand	founding
			expansionism	unfounded
			expansive	
			expandable	

Exercise - Word Form Chart

NOUN	VERB	ADJECTIVE	ADVERB
1. chart	1. *chart*	1. *charted* 2. *uncharted*	
1. *encounter*	1. encounter		
1. *ethics*		1. ethical 2. *unethical*	1. *ethically*
1. expansion 2. *expansionism*	1. *expand*	1. *expanded* 2. *expanding* 3. *expansive* 4. *expandable*	
1. *founder*	1. found	1. *founder* 2. *founding* 3. *unfounder*	

B. READING

Mistakes in the New World

In the 15th and 16th centuries, Europe sent many explorers to the "new world" to find new territories for economic expansion. These first explorers made a detailed chart of each newly discovered area, and eventually many European settlements were founded in North and South America. When native cultures encountered European explorers it usually ended badly for the natives, and this mistreatment and displacement of large groups of native people has raised many ethical questions among historians in recent years. Actions that seemed "right" to the explorers of the time now appear to many to be unacceptable and immoral.

C. COMPREHENSION CHECK
Exercise 1
Refer to the reading above and use the context to guess the meanings of the words below. Then match the words to their definitions. Do NOT use a dictionary.

C 1. chart
E 2. expansion
A 3. encountered
B 4. ethical
D 5. founded

A. met by chance
B. morally correct
C. map or display of information
D. established, started
E. growth, increase

Exercise 2
Circle the word that does not belong.

1. map / chart / display / (chair)
2. expansion / enlargement / (discussion) / growth
3. (sinful) / ethical / correct / moral
4. began / founded / established / (attacked)
5. confrontations / (deliveries) / meetings / encounters

D. WORD STUDY
Exercise 1

> **Literal versus figurative meanings** – The exact meaning of a word is its literal meaning. However, some words can also have a figurative usage. This means that the word is used more imaginatively to express the meaning in a comparative or metaphorical way.
>
> For example, if we say "North America was <u>uncharted territory</u> when Christopher Columbus first saw it", the expression "uncharted territory" literally means that there were no maps or sources of geographical information about the place. Now, imagine a completely different situation. Imagine that you are going to go on a "blind date". This means that you are going to go out for the evening with someone you have never met before. You might feel nervous about being in <u>un charted territory</u> with this person. In this case, the expression means "in an unpredictable situation" and has nothing to do with maps or charts.

Think about a time when you went into uncharted territory (figuratively). On a separate piece of paper, write a short paragraph about the causes and effects of this situation. Then exchange your paper with other classmates.

Write a few sentences.

Exercise 2

Study the multiple meanings and uses of the words below. Then do the exercise that follows.

> 1. founded (v) -   established, started
>
> 2. founded (adj.) -   based on something solid, having validity
>   (opposite: unfounded)

> 3. **expandable versus expansive - Expandable** means physically capable of being enlarged or stretched out. **Expansive** means emotionally friendly, open, and generous ("to be in an expansive mood").

Fill in the blanks with the correct vocabulary word (**founded, unfounded, expandable, expansive**).

1. The husband's accusation of infidelity was _unfounded_ . There was no evidence that his wife had had an affair.

2. I like folders that are _expandable_ so I can add more papers easily.

3. Zachary was feeling so _expansive_ after winning the award that he offered to buy everyone dinner.

4. Christine's research paper contained well _founded_ conclusions.

5. The university was _founded_ in 1850 by Fred Smith.

E. USING WORDS IN COMMUNICATION
Exercise

1. List 3 difficult <u>ethical</u> decisions that face many people.

2. List 3 things that you consider to be <u>unethical</u>.

3. List 3 subjects that you would enjoy studying just to <u>expand</u> your knowledge.

REVIEW

Unscramble each of the vocabulary words from this unit.
Then use the marked letters to solve the second puzzle.

CIHALTE — e t h i c a l (12)

UMIEDM — m e d i u m (20)

EPTYOARMR — t e m p o r a r y (19, 5, 18)

NTAOTCC — c o n t a c t (6)

EUTRCNENO — e n c o u n t e r (2)

RRIRATABY — a r b i t r a r y (7)

CIIATEATLF — f a c i l i t a t e (1)

NGGOONI — o n g o i n g (4)

LBKU — b u l k (8)

HMNIIIDS — d i m i n i s h (14)

MPNOUDCO — c o m p o u n d (13)

EODDFNU — f o u n d e d (3)

TIPONRO — p o r t i o n (11)

TACHR — c h a r t (10)

DPNIXPEA — a p p e n d i x

HGSNIIT — i n s i g h t (15)

TACUTRENL — r e l u c t a n t (9)

SSALALICC — c l a s s i c a l

IPENONAXS — e x p a n s i o n (17)

MEAUTR — m a t u r e (16)

C o n g r a t u l a t i o n s   t o   y o u
1 2 3 4 5 6 7 8 9 10 11 12 13 14 15   16 17   18 19 20

UNIT 4

WORDS

adjacent	currency	inherent	preliminary
analogy	deviate	manual	revolution
cease	enormous	nonetheless	rigid
coincide	erode	norm	supplement
convince	format	overlap	undergo

READINGS

Earth Friendly Farming
Women's Roles
Acceptance of New Technology
Economic Crisis

STRATEGIES AND SKILLS

Word Forms
- ▫ Word family chart
- ▫ Word form selection

Comprehension Check
- ▫ Matching definitions
- ▫ Identifying synonyms
- ▫ Understanding words in context

Word Expansion
- ▫ Multiple meanings
- ▫ Grammar application
- ▫ Analogies

Interactive Speaking Practice
- ▫ Discussion
- ▫ Listing
- ▫ Application

ACADEMIC WORD POWER

LESSON 1

A. WORD FAMILIES

Study the five word families below. Then fill in the word form chart. The underlined word forms at the top of the list are the most commonly used forms in academic texts.

adjacent	cease	convince	erode	manual (2X)
/ə ˈdʒeɪsənt/	/sis/	/kən ˈvɪns/	/ɪ ˈroʊd/	/ˈmænyuəl/
	ceaseless	convincing	erosion	manually
		unconvincing	eroded	
		convincingly	eroding	
		unconvinced		
		convinced		

Exercise - Word Form Chart

NOUN	VERB	ADJECTIVE	ADVERB
		1. adjacent	
	1. cease	1.	
	1. convince	1. 2. 3. 4.	1.
1.	1. erode	1. 2.	
1. manual		1.	1.

B. READING

Earth Friendly Farming

The agriculture specialist <u>convinced</u> the farmer to <u>cease</u> cutting down trees and clearing away bushes on the hills <u>adjacent</u> to his fields by explaining that removing foliage and ground cover from the area would cause the soil to <u>erode</u> and eventually result in mudslides or flooding. He also gave the farmer a <u>manual</u> full of facts and advice about wise farming techniques.

C. COMPREHENSION CHECK
Exercise 1

Refer to the reading above and use the context to guess the meanings of the words below. Then match the words to their definitions. Do NOT use a dictionary.

___ 1. adjacent	A. wear or wash away, weaken
___ 2. cease	B. next to
___ 3. convinced	C. stop
___ 4. erode	D. guidebook with step by step procedures
___ 5. manual	E. persuaded

Exercise 2
Circle the word that doesn't belong.

1. weaken	wash away	improve	erode
2. convinced	disagreed	persuaded	coaxed
3. handbook	newspaper	manual	guidebook
4. beside	next to	adjacent	between
5. stop	cease	continue	halt

D. WORD STUDY
Exercise
Study the multiple meanings and uses of the vocabulary words, and then do the exercise that follows.

> 1. erode (v) - physically deteriorate, wear down, wash away over time
>
> 2. erode (v) - weaken or lessen the strength or power of something

> 3. manual (n) - a guidebook with step by step procedures
>
> 4. manual (adj) - done by using the hands rather than a machine

Write YES if the underlined word is used correctly, or write NO if it is used incorrectly.

_____ 1. Paul's feelings of trust quickly eroded after his girlfriend lied to him.

_____ 2. Men who do manual labor usually wear a suit and tie to work.

_____ 3. The strong wind last night caused the roof to erode off the house.

_____ 4. Many people prefer to drive a car with a manual transmission because they think they are not really in full control if their car has an automatic transmission.

E. USING WORDS IN COMMUNICATION
Exercise
With a partner discuss the following questions.

1. Describe the people who live in the apartment or house adjacent to yours.

2. What are some factors that might cause a friendship to erode?

3. What are your least favorite manual household chores? Why?

4. How would you go about convincing your friend to cease his/her heavy drinking?

LESSON 2

A. WORD FAMILIES

Study the five word families below. Then fill in the word form chart. The underlined word forms at the top of the list are the most commonly used forms in academic texts.

analogous	inherent	revolution	rigid	undergo
/ə ˈnæləgəs/	/ɪn ˈhɛrənt/	/ˌrɛvə ˈluʃən/	/ ˈrɪdʒɪd/	/ˌʌndər ˈgoʊ/
analogy	inherently	revolutionary (2X)	rigidity	
		revolutionize	rigidly	
		revolutionized		
		revolutionizing		

Exercise - Word Form Chart

NOUN	VERB	ADJECTIVE	ADVERB
1.		1. analogous	
		1. inherent	1.
1. revolution 2.	1.	1. 2. 3.	
1.		1. rigid	1.
	1. undergo		

B. READING

Women's Roles

Post World War II American culture was based on strong family values. The traditional family structure was <u>analogous</u> to safety and security for those who had experienced fear and uncertainty during the war years. Although many women had held down full time responsible jobs while the men were off fighting the war, the stay-at-home wife and mother became <u>inherent</u> in the family structure of the 1950s. By the early 1960s however, women had begun to question this <u>rigid</u> definition of their role in the world, and in the years that followed, the United States <u>underwent</u> a huge women's liberation <u>revolution</u> that resulted in major changes both in the home and in the workplace.

C. COMPREHENSION CHECK
Exercise 1

Refer to the reading above and use the context to guess the meanings of the words below. Then match the words to their definitions. Do NOT use a dictionary.

___ 1. inherent   A. a big change
___ 2. analogous   B. stiff, difficult to bend
___ 3. rigid   C. experienced
___ 4. underwent   D. naturally belonging to or part of
___ 5. revolution   E. similar, nearly the same

Exercise 2
Write YES if the underlined word is used correctly or NO if it is not used correctly.

_____ 1. Easy access to computers has brought about a telecommunications <u>revolution</u>.

_____ 2. The university admissions board considered a score of 90% on their own entrance exam to be <u>analogous</u> to a 550 on the paper TOEFL.

_____ 3. Disloyalty is <u>inherent</u> in a good relationship.

_____ 4. Mrs. Brown did not like to follow a <u>rigid</u> schedule, so she didn't own any clocks or watches!

_____ 5. The subway line <u>underwent</u> the downtown area of the city.

D. WORD STUDY
Exercise 1
Many words in English are commonly used with certain prepositions. Find these words (or forms of these words) in the reading and write the prepositions that go with them on the line provided. (Hint: one of the words has no collocating preposition.)

1. inherent _____
2. undergo _____
3. analogous _____

Exercise 2
An **analogy** is a statement of a relationship between two or more things. Analogy making is tested on some entrance exams such as the GRE. Study the basic formation of the analogies below and then do the exercise that follows.

> **Analogies** are usually presented in the following way: **A : B :: 1 : 2**
> This is read "A is to B in the same way that 1 is to 2" (or "A is to B as 1 is to 2").
> Each pair of words has a similar relationship.
>
> For example, if the first pair of words are antonyms (big : small), then the second pair will also be antonyms (heavy : light)

Try to complete the following analogies:

1. difficult : easy :: rigid : _____
2. cease : stop :: undergo : _____
3. rigid : stiff :: analogous : _____
4. inherent : belonging :: revolution: _____

E. USING WORDS IN COMMUNICATION
Exercise

1. List 3 changes your life has <u>undergone</u> in the last year.

2. List 3 rules in your family, work or school that you think are too <u>rigid</u>.

3. List 3 qualities that are <u>inherent</u> to a successful marriage.

LESSON 3

A. WORD FAMILIES

Study the five word families below. Then fill in the word form chart. The underlined word forms at the top of the list are the most commonly used forms in academic texts.

coincide	deviation	format (2X)	norm	preliminary
/koʊɪn ˈsaɪd/	/ˌdivi ˈeɪʃən/	/ ˈfɔr ˌmæt/	/nɔrm/	/prɪ ˈlɪmə ˌnɛri/
coincidence	deviate	formatted		preliminaries
coinciding	deviating			
coincidental	deviant (2X)			
coincidentally				

Exercise - Word Form Chart

NOUN	VERB	ADJECTIVE	ADVERB
1.	1. coincide	1. 2.	1.
1. deviation 2.	1.	1. 2.	
1. format	1.	1.	
1. norm			
1.		1. preliminary	

B. READING

Acceptance of New Technology

Jeff's sociology research project has undergone important changes since he set up the preliminary format three months ago. At first, his plan involved doing a completely new experiment about attitudes concerning computers, but later he decided to redo a study that had been done in the 1950s about acceptance of new technology. He wanted to see if people's attitudes now would coincide with the views of those questioned 50 years ago. He predicted that there would not be a significant deviation from the norms established in the earlier study.

C. COMPREHENSION CHECK
Exercise 1

Refer to the reading above and use the context to guess the meanings of the words below. Then match the words to their definitions. Do NOT use a dictionary.

    ___ 1. preliminary   A. agree

    ___ 2. format   B. a general arrangement of something

    ___ 3. coincide   C. averages, expected results

    ___ 4. deviation   D. a difference from what is expected

    ___ 5. norms   E. related to preparation

Exercise 2

Write T for true or F for false in the blanks.

_____ 1. The <u>norm</u> on a test is usually a grade of C.

_____ 2. Snow in Florida in July would be a <u>deviation</u> in weather patterns.

_____ 3. If I choose "True" and you choose "False", our answers <u>coincide</u>.

_____ 4. The <u>format</u> of this book includes 4 lessons in each unit.

_____ 5. Athletes should do some <u>preliminary</u> stretching exercises after a game.

D. WORD STUDY

Exercise 1

Many words in English are commonly used with certain prepositions. Find these words (or forms of these words) in the reading and write the prepositions that go with them on the line provided. (Hint: one of the words has no collocating preposition.)

1. norms   _____
2. coincide   _____
3. deviate   _____

Write your own sentences using the 2 collocations.

1. _____

    _____

2. _____

    _____

Exercise 2

Study the multiple meanings of the words below, and then do the exercise that follows.

> 1. coincide (v) - to be in agreement
> 2. coincide (v) - to happen at the same time (Note: The noun form for this meaning is **coincidence**. Thus, a coincidence is the happening of two or more events at the same time by chance.)

> 3. norms (n) - averages, expected results
> 4. norms (n) - rules of expected behavior in a culture

Match the beginning and ending clauses to form a sentence. Write the letters for the second clauses in the blanks.

_____ 1. His grade of 78   A. <u>coincides</u> with my opinion of them.

_____ 2. His dislike of cigars   B. would probably be a <u>coincidence</u>.

_____ 3. My arrival in Boston   C. violates the <u>norms</u> for the occasion.

_____ 4. Wearing shorts to a wedding   D. matches the <u>norms</u> for the test.

_____ 5. Two colleagues wearing the same sweater to work   E. <u>coincides</u> with his departure.

E. USING WORDS IN COMMUNICATION
Exercise

Norms vary from culture to culture and many misunderstandings can result from not knowing how another culture's norms differ from your own.

Imagine you are a tour guide in the United States, working with tourists from around the world. Make one list of behaviors that tourists should avoid doing while visiting the United States and another list of behaviors that they will be expected to do while in the United States. Compare your list with a classmate's list.

<u>Behaviors to avoid</u>   <u>Behaviors that are expected</u>

LESSON 4

A. WORD FAMILIES

Study the five word families below. Then fill in the word form chart. The underlined word forms at the top of the list are the most commonly used forms in academic texts.

currency	enormous	nonetheless	overlap (2X)	supplementary
/ˈkɛrənsi/	/ɪˈnɔrməs/	/ˌnʌnðəˈlɛs/	/ˌouvərˈlæp/	/ˌsʌpləˈmɛntəri/
	enormity		overlapped	supplement (2X)
	enormously		overlapping	

Exercise - Word Form Chart

NOUN	VERB	ADJECTIVE	ADVERB
1. currency			
1.		1. enormous	1.
			1. nonetheless
1.	1. overlap	1. 2.	
1.	1.	1. supplementary	

B. READING

Economic Crisis

In the late 1990s, a sudden devaluation of the <u>currency</u> of several Asian countries caused <u>enormous</u> problems for many Asian students studying in the United States. Because the exchange rate on the money from their parents left them with fewer dollars than before, many students had to find part time jobs to get a <u>supplementary</u> income. Unfortunately, their work hours sometimes <u>overlapped</u> their scheduled class times causing them to miss classes once in a while. <u>Nonetheless</u>, most students succeeded in balancing their work and study schedules and went on to graduate in their chosen fields.

C. COMPREHENSION CHECK
Exercise 1
Refer to the reading above and use the context to guess the meanings of the words below. Then match the words to their definitions. Do NOT use a dictionary.

___ 1. currency	A. huge
___ 2. enormous	B. happened partly at the same time, coincided
___ 3. nonetheless	C. money used in a country
___ 4. overlapped	D. in spite of that
___ 5. supplementary	E. extra, additional

Exercise 2
Circle the word that does not belong.

1. coin   currency   present   bill
2. large   huge   dull   enormous
3. however   nevertheless   nonetheless   therefore
4. manage   coincide   overlap   coexist
5. supplementary flexible   added   extra

D. WORD STUDY
Exercise 1
Study the multiple uses and meanings for the vocabulary words below and then do the exercise that follows.

1. currency (n) - money used to pay for goods or services in a country

2. currency (n) - wide acceptance, relevance

3. overlap (v) - to have part of one object over another, to cover something partly

4. overlap (v) - to coincide

Fill in the blank with the correct vocabulary word (**currency, overlap**) and write the number of the correct meaning in the first blank. You may need to change verb tenses.

____ 1. By coincidence, my visit to Paris _____ my friend's vacation in France, so we made plans to meet for dinner near the Seine one night.

____ 2. At first the _____ of another country can be confusing because the coins and bills may be of different shapes and sizes.

____ 3. That conservative politician's ideas have little _____ among the students at that liberal arts college.

____ 4. Marge's sweater _____ her pants, so she didn't need to wear a belt.

Exercise 2

Refer to the Word Form Chart at the beginning of this lesson and choose the vocabulary word that fits into each of the following sentences.

1. In addition to his retirement pay from his former workplace, the 80-year-old also received a Social Security _____ from the government.

2. Francis was _____ relieved when the library security guard found the backpack which contained her only copy of her research paper.

3. Greg was exhausted; _____ , he had to stay at work until he finished the project.

E. USING WORDS IN COMMUNICATION
Exercise
Share your ideas with a partner.

1. Describe the <u>currency</u> of your country. Explain the size, shape, color and value of all the different coins and bills.

2. What kind of part time jobs would you be willing to do to <u>supplement</u> your income?

3. In addition to attending an English class, what are some useful <u>supplementary</u> activities that will help you to improve your English?

REVIEW

Choose any five words from this unit and write one in each oval. Then write any four words that you associate with those words on the extending lines. Be able to explain your associations to a partner. (See the example to the right.)

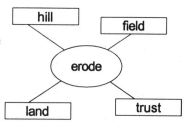

1.

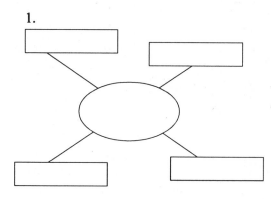

2.

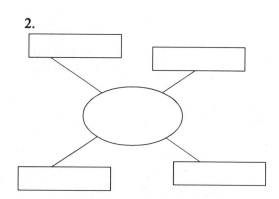

3.

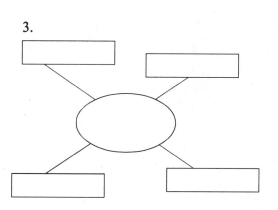

4.

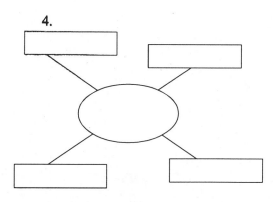

5.

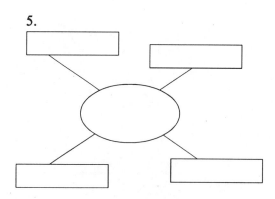

UNIT 5

WORDS

accommodation	displacement	levy	refine
behalf	forthcoming	military	so-called
commence	incompatible	odds	subordinate
compile	induce	passive	unify
device	inevitably	pose	vision

READINGS

Army Aggravation
Declare or Beware!
Thinking Outside the Box
A Helping Hand

STRATEGIES AND SKILLS

Word Forms
  □ Word family chart
  □ Word form selection
Comprehension Check
  □ Matching definitions
  □ Understanding and using words in context
  □ Identifying synonyms
Word Expansion
  □ Multiple meanings
  □ Collocations
Interactive Speaking Practice
  □ Discussion
  □ Associations
  □ Summarizing

ACADEMIC WORD POWER

LESSON 1

A. WORD FAMILIES

Study the five word families below. Then fill in the word form chart. The underlined word forms at the top of the list are the most commonly used forms in academic texts.

incompatible	induce	military (2X)	odds	subordinate (2X)
/ˌɪnkəmˈpætəbəl/	/ɪnˈdus/	/ ˈmɪləˌtɛri/	/ɑdz /	/sə ˈbɔrdnɪt/
compatible	induced		odd	subordinates
compatibility	induction			subordination
incompatibility	inducing			

Exercise - Word Form Chart

NOUN	VERB	ADJECTIVE	ADVERB
1. 2.		1. incompatible 2.	
1.	1. induce	1. 2.	
1.		1. military	
1. odds		1.	
1. 2.	1.	1. subordinate	

B. READING

Army Aggravation

Jason's father was able to <u>induce</u> him to join the army by telling him that <u>military</u> service would provide him with not only education and training but also great new experiences and adventures. Unfortunately, Jason soon found that his independent personality was <u>incompatible</u> with the rules and regulations of army life. He rejected his <u>subordinate</u> status and was constantly in trouble with his commanding officers. The <u>odds</u> of his wanting to reenlist are very slim indeed!

C. COMPREHENSION CHECK
Exercise 1
Refer to the reading above and use the context to guess the meanings of the words below. Then match the words to their definitions. Do NOT use a dictionary.

___ 1. induce	A. not able to work or be together
___ 2. military	B. chances, likelihood
___ 3. incompatible	C. make someone do something, persuade, coax
___ 4. subordinate	D. connected to the armed forces of a nation
___ 5. odds	E. of lower rank, not as important

Exercise 2
Write YES if the underlined word is used correctly or NO if it is used incorrectly.

_____ 1. Her clothes are <u>odds</u>. I've never seen anything like them!

_____ 2. Colleen and her husband of one year are getting divorced because they are <u>incompatible</u>.

_____ 3. The coach tried to <u>induce</u> the football team to play even harder during the second half of the game.

_____ 4. A king is the <u>subordinate</u> of a prince.

_____ 5. John joined the <u>military</u> service because he wanted to fight in the war.

D. WORD STUDY
Exercise 1
Some words have more than one commonly used meaning or are easily confused with similar words. Look at the examples below. Then do the exercise that follows.

---

1. (in)compatible (adj) - (psychological) refers to (not) getting along well in a relationship (work, personal, etc.)

2. (in)compatible (adj) - (physical) refers to (not) functioning properly together because components are (not) made to go together

---

3. induce (v) - to induce someone to do something = coax or persuade

4. induce (v) - to induce a feeling or action = to bring out or cause

---

5. odds (n) - "the odds of something happening" = the chances or probability of something happening

6. odds (n) - to succeed "against the odds" = against the expected or likely outcome

7. odds (n) - "to be at odds with" = to be in a conflicting position, not getting along with

8. odds (n) - "odds and ends" = small extra items

9. odd (adj) - unusual, not what is usually expected

Cross out the items (words or expressions) that DO NOT go with the underlined word(s). In each list, one or two items may be crossed out.

1. Odds and ends include	pencils and pens. cars and boats. stamps and paper clips. textbooks and notebooks. rubber bands and glue.	

2.	Patriotism Jewelry Anxiety Vomiting	can be induced.

3. You might be at odds with	a neighbor. a new pair of shoes. your business partner. an economic policy. your teacher.	

4.	Snow in Tahiti A test at the end of a term A person with 12 fingers A car with no steering wheel A child wearing shoes	would be considered odd.

5.	Oil and water Cats and dogs Ex-friends A TV and a VCR A cassette and a CD player	are usually considered to be incompatible.

Exercise 2

Sometimes words that are spelled the same way have different pronunciations based on the word form. Look at this example.

> 1. subordin**ate** (n or adj) – the **ate** ending sounds like "it."
>
> 2. subordin**ate** (v) – the **ate** ending sounds like "ate."

Sometimes words must be used in a specific collocation. Look at this example.

> military - This word can be used as an adjective or as a noun. However, when it is used as a noun, it is always preceded by "the" as in the military. This means the military forces.

E. USING WORDS IN COMMUNICATION
Exercise
Discuss the following with a partner.

1. Do you have an <u>odds</u> and ends drawer at home? What's in it?

2. What are the <u>odds</u> that you will have one million dollars in ten years?

3. Have you ever done <u>military</u> service, or do you plan to? How do you feel about being treated as a <u>subordinate</u>?

4. What kind of people do you feel <u>compatible</u> with? What kind of people would you expect to be <u>incompatible</u> with?

LESSON 2

A. WORD FAMILIES

Study the five word families below. Then fill in the word form chart. The underlined word forms at the top of the list are the most commonly used forms in academic texts.

<u>commence</u>	<u>compile</u> (2X)	<u>device</u>	<u>forthcoming</u>	<u>levy</u> (2X)
/kəˈmɛns/	/kəmˈpaɪl/	/dɪˈvaɪs/	/fɔrθˈkʌmɪŋ/	/ˈlɛvi/
commencement	compilation			
recommence				

Exercise - Word Form Chart

NOUN	VERB	ADJECTIVE	ADVERB
1.	1. commence 2.		
1.	1. compile		
1. device			
		1. forthcoming	
1.	1. levy		

B. READING

Declare or Beware!

When Janet's flight from Singapore landed in Los Angeles, Janet had already filled out her immigration forms and had <u>compiled</u> a list of items she had purchased while overseas. However, when she went through customs, the agent <u>commenced</u> a thorough search of her luggage and found several things that she had not declared. Since Janet was not very <u>forthcoming</u> with a reasonable explanation, the agent took out a special <u>device</u> for calculating the value of the goods so that he could <u>levy</u> a large fine. Janet's vacation did not have a happy ending!

C. COMPREHENSION CHECK
Exercise 1

Refer to the reading above and use the context to guess the meanings of the words below.
    Then match the words to their definitions. Do NOT use a dictionary.

____ 1. compile	A.	began
____ 2. commenced	B.	put together item by item
____ 3. forthcoming	C.	a tool, electrical or mechanical machine
____ 4. device	D.	helpful, cooperative
____ 5. levy	E.	to require to pay a fee, such as taxes or custom duties

Exercise 2
Circle the word that does not belong.

1. tax	levy	lift	fine
2. forthcoming	arriving	open	helpful
3. gathered	divided	collected	compiled
4. feeling	mechanism	device	tool
5. began	commenced	started	praised

D. WORD STUDY
Exercise 1
Study the multiple meanings and uses of the vocabulary words, and then do the exercise that follows.

> 1. device (n) - (concrete) tool, electrical or mechanical machine
>
> 2. device (n) - (abstract) secret or clever means to an end

> 3. forthcoming (adj) - helpful, cooperative
>
> 4. forthcoming (adj) - arriving in the future
>
> 5. forthcoming (adj) - willing to provide information (usually used in the negative, i.e. not forthcoming)

> 6. commencement (n) - the beginning of something
>
> 7. commencement (n) - a graduation ceremony

Write YES if the underlined word is used correctly or NO if it is used incorrectly.

_____ 1. Beginning a lecture with a question is a common <u>device</u> to catch the students' attention.

_____ 2. After two weeks of rain, everyone hopes sunny weather will be <u>forthcoming</u>.

_____ 3. The <u>device</u> used to tie your shoes is called a shoelace.

_____ 4. My sister sang a song at her <u>commencement</u> ceremony.

E. USING WORDS IN COMMUNICATION
Exercise
Discuss these topics in small groups.

1. Tell about a time in your life when you were not <u>forthcoming</u> – when you were not willing to provide information to someone.

2. Think of several <u>devices</u> that you use every day. Rank them in order of their importance to you, and explain this ranking to your group.

3. Did you attend a high school <u>commencement</u> ceremony? Describe it.

4. Do you often make lists? What kind of things do you like to <u>compile</u>?

LESSON 3

A. WORD FAMILIES

Study the five word families below. Then fill in the word form chart. The underlined word forms at the top of the list are the most commonly used forms in academic texts.

<u>pose</u> (2X)	<u>refine</u>	<u>so-called</u>	<u>unify</u>	<u>vision</u>
/pouz/	/rɪˈfaɪn/	/soʊkɔld/	/ˈyunəˌfaɪ/	/vɪdʒən/
posed	refinement		unified	
posing	refined		unification	
	refining		unifying	

Exercise - Word Form Chart

NOUN	VERB	ADJECTIVE	ADVERB
1.	1. pose	1. 2.	
1.	1. refine	1. 2.	
		1. so-called	
1.	1. unify	1. 2.	
1. vision			

B. READING

Thinking Outside the Box

The top executives of the company met with the CEO to set new goals for the coming decade and also to <u>refine</u> existing company standards. There was general agreement that the company's management style had become old fashioned and fragmented. They discussed ways to <u>unify</u> the management standards based on a more modern <u>vision</u>. One of the female executives <u>posed</u> a question about the <u>so-called</u> "glass ceiling," a perceived block to promoting women to top management positions, and suggested that removing this barrier be made one of the primary goals for the company.

C. COMPREHENSION CHECK

Exercise 1

Refer to the reading above and use the context to guess the meanings of the words below. Then match the words to their definitions. Do NOT use a dictionary.

___ 1. refine	A.	presented a question or an idea
___ 2. unify	B.	change, improve
___ 3. vision	C.	usually known as
___ 4. posed	D.	bring together as a whole, integrated
___ 5. so-called	E.	foresight, ability to see into the future

Exercise 2
True or False? Write T or F in the blanks.

___ 1. When you wave the <u>so-called</u> stars and stripes, you are waving a U.S. flag.

___ 2. East and West Berlin were <u>unified</u> after World War II, and a wall was built between them.

___ 3. In the middle of a class, you should raise your hand before you <u>pose</u> a question.

___ 4. After you write the first draft of your essay, you should go back and <u>refine</u> your ideas.

___ 5. People who know what they want to do next weekend have great <u>vision</u>.

D. WORD STUDY
Exercise
Study the multiple meanings and uses of the vocabulary words, and then do the exercise that follows.

---

1. pose (transitive verb) - ask a question or put forth an idea

2. pose (intransitive verb) - model in a stationary position for a photo or painting

3. pose (intransitive verb + as) - pretend to be

---

4. refine (v) - (physical) remove impurities, process from a raw state

5. refine (v) - (cultural) make more sophisticated, educate in etiquette

6. refine (v) - (communicative) make ideas clearer, better

---

7. vision (n) - (abstract) foresight, dream

8. vision (n) - (physical) ability to see, sight

---

9. so-called (adj) - usually known as

10. so-called (adj) - incorrectly known as

Match the clauses on the left with those that complete them on the right. Write the letters of the completion in the blanks.

____ 1. The young man <u>posed</u>

A. had great <u>vision</u> and imagination.

____ 2. Most nutritionists agree that fresh produce is better than

B. an ideal solution to her company's shipping problem.

____ 3. The children <u>posed</u>

C. to have my <u>vision</u> checked.

____ 4. I've made an appointment with the eye doctor

D. as a doctor even though he never went to medical school.

____ 5. Lady Diana underwent rigorous training

E. <u>refined</u> foods that come in cans and packages.

____ 6. The quietest member of the committee suddenly <u>posed</u>

F. <u>refined</u> the contributor's writing to suit the readers' taste.

____ 7. Michelangelo, a 15th century artist who drew airplanes,

G. for a portrait with their mother.

____ 8. The magazine editor

H. involved rescuing a cat from a tree.

____ 9. We were surprised to find out that his <u>so-called</u> act of heroism

I. to learn the <u>refined</u> behavior expected of royalty.

E. USING WORDS IN COMMUNICATION
Exercise
Associations - On a separate piece of paper, make three lists using the words
refined, unified, and **posed**. Write at least five words you associate with these words in each list. Then cut up the lists and see if your partner can put the lists back together again.

LESSON 4

A. WORD FAMILIES

Study the five word families below. Then fill in the word form chart. The underlined word forms at the top of the list are the most commonly used forms in academic texts.

accommodation	behalf	displacement	inevitably	passive
/əˌkɑməˈdeɪʃən/	/bɪˈhæf/	/dɪsˈpleɪmɛnt/	/ɪnˈɛvətəbəl/	/ˈpæsɪv/
accommodate		displace	inevitable	passively
accommodating		displaced	inevitability	

Exercise - Word Form Chart

NOUN	VERB	ADJECTIVE	ADVERB
1. accommodation	1.	1.	
1. behalf			
1. displacement	1.	1.	
1.		1.	1. inevitably
		1. passive	1.

B. READING

A Helping Hand

The United Nations High Commissioner for Refugees (UNHCR) is an international organization that provides assistance for refugees around the world. When large groups of people flee their homes due to war or natural disaster, the first consequence of their <u>displacement</u> is a lack of <u>accommodations</u>. The UNHCR sets up tent cities and also provides food, clothing and medical attention for the refugees. At first, these people are often in shock and display a <u>passive</u> acceptance of the aid provided on their <u>behalf.</u> However, after a brief time, they <u>inevitably</u> become anxious to regain control of and responsibility for their own lives.

C. COMPREHENSION CHECK
Exercise 1
Refer to the reading above and use the context to guess the meanings of the words below. Then match the words to their definitions. Do NOT use a dictionary.

___ 1. displacement   A. lodging, housing arrangement

___ 2. accommodations   B. as a representative, for the benefit

___ 3. passive   C. removal, making into a refugee

___ 4. behalf   D. unavoidably, definitely going to happen

___ 5. inevitably   E. accepting without resistance, unwilling to act

Exercise 2
Use the vocabulary words from Exercise 1 to fill in the blanks.

1. The conference organizers provided free _____ for the speakers.

2. If you continue to overeat, you will _____ gain weight.

3. Gandhi taught that _____ resistance was better than violence.

4. Sandra was ill, so her colleague attended the meeting on her _____ .

5. The _____ of Native Americans from their traditional lands to reservations caused great hardships.

D. WORD STUDY
Exercise
Some words have more than one meaning and also change meaning when they change form or are used in different collocations. Look at the following examples.

1. accommodations (n) - lodging, rooms and other facilities

2. accommodations (n) - arrangements made for someone

3. accommodate (v) - to have enough space

4. accommodate (v) - to make an extra effort to do what one asks

5. accommodating (adj) - helpful, cooperative

---

6. displacement (n) - the act of changing the place or position

7. displacement (n) - (chemistry) a reaction where one kind of atom or molecule is removed and replaced by another

8. displacement (n) - (physics) the weight or volume of a liquid displaced by a floating object

9. displacement (n) - (psychology) the shifting of an emotion (like anger) from an appropriate to an inappropriate object.

---

10. behalf (n) - on behalf of = as a representative of

11. behalf (n) - in behalf of = for the benefit of

Write YES if the underlined word or phrase is used correctly or NO if it is used incorrectly.

_____ 1. Gail is such an <u>accommodating</u> person. She loves to stay in hotels.

_____ 2. The students donated canned food <u>in behalf of</u> the tornado victims.

_____ 3. The teacher made <u>accommodations</u> for the hospitalized student to take the exam at a later date.

_____ 4. The psychoanalyst felt that the patient's <u>displacement</u> of her anger about her own childhood onto her children was potentially dangerous.

_____ 5. Laura spent 10 hours in the library <u>on behalf of</u> her research paper.

E. USING WORDS IN COMMUNICATION
Exercise

Reread the reading at the beginning of this lesson. Then close your book. Without looking at the reading, give your partner a summary of the reading using as many of the vocabulary words as you can.

REVIEW

Circle words and draw lines between words that you associate with each other. There is not one correct word association, and you may have more than one association with certain words and no associations at all with other words. Think about why you make these associations, and be able to explain them to a partner.

accommodation   displacement

                        levy

refine   behalf

                        forthcoming

military   so-called

                        commenced

incompatible   odds

                        subordinate

compiled   induce

                        passive

unified   device

                        posed

inevitably   vision

UNIT 6

WORDS

assurance	depression	invoke	qualitative
coherence	devote	minimal	restraint
collapse	exploitation	nuclear	specify
commodity	infrastructure	persistent	straightforward
confine	intrinsic	procedure	violation

READINGS

Protecting Patients' Rights
Nuclear Power: Opposing Sides
A Marketing Strategy
Following the Law

STRATEGIES AND SKILLS

Word Forms
- Word family chart
- Word form selection

Comprehension Check
- Matching definitions
- Identifying synonyms
- Understanding and using words in context

Word Expansion
- Collocations
- Multiple meaning

Interactive Speaking Practice
- Discussion
- Summarizing
- Synthesis

ACADEMIC WORD POWER

LESSON 1

A. WORD FAMILIES

Study the five word families below. Then fill in the word form chart. The underlined word forms at the top of the list are the most commonly used forms in academic texts.

coherence	confine	depression	exploitation	persistent
/koʊˈhɪrəns/	/kənˈfaɪn/	/dɪˈprɛʃən/	/ˌɛksplɔɪˈteɪʃən/	/pərˈsɪstənt/
coherent	confined	depress	exploit	persist
coherently	confining	depressing	exploited	persistence
incoherent	unconfined	depressed	exploiting	persistently
incoherently				

Exercise - Word Form Chart

NOUN	VERB	ADJECTIVE	ADVERB
1. coherence		1. 2.	1. 2.
	1. confine	1. 2. 3.	
1. depression	1.	1. 2.	
1. exploitation	1.	1. 2.	
1.	1.	1. persistent	1.

B. READING

Protecting Patients' Rights

Some people suffer from severe, <u>persistent</u> <u>depression</u>. Their feelings of sadness and hopelessness may continue and worsen until it becomes necessary to <u>confine</u> them in a mental institution for their own safety. This would seem to be the right thing to do, but the authorities must be careful to ensure that confined patients maintain some personal rights. For example, if patients are given so many drugs that they become totally passive and completely lacking in <u>coherence</u>, it could be considered <u>exploitation</u> by the institution.

C. COMPREHENSION CHECK
Exercise 1
Refer to the reading above and use the context to guess the meanings of the words below. Then match the words to their definitions. Do NOT use a dictionary.

___ 1. persistent	A. clarity and logic, clear-headedness
___ 2. depression	B. unfair treatment, taking advantage of in a bad way
___ 3. confine	C. feeling of sadness, mental illness
___ 4. coherence	D. continuing to exist for a long time
___ 5. exploitation	E. to keep within certain limits, restrict

Exercise 2
Circle the word that does not belong.

1. coherence	adhesive	logic	clearness
2. continuing	persistent	chronic	existing
3. restricted	informed	limited	confined
4. recreation	sadness	hopelessness	depression
5. misuse	exploitation	mistreatment	rejection

D. WORD STUDY
Exercise
Choose the correct word form for each blank.

1. Caroline's presentation was well received because she spoke so _____ about her topic.
   a. coherence   b. coherent   c. coherently   d. incoherent

2. I hate to wear high boots! I find them to be too _____ !
   a. confine   b. confined   c. unconfined   d. confining

3. Who wants to pay money to see that movie? It's too _____ .
   a. depression   b. depressing   c. depressed   d. depress

4. The _____ factory workers complained to the police.
   a. exploited   b. exploiting   c. exploitation   d. exploit

5. Martha should go to see a doctor about her _____ cough.
   a. persistently   b. persist   c. persistence   d. persistent

E. USING WORDS IN COMMUNICATION
Exercise
Discuss the following with a partner.

1. What could you say or do to help a _depressed_ friend? What would you do if you thought that person might hurt him or herself?

2. When you are in a _confined_ space (like an elevator or a tunnel) does it bother you? Do you know someone who is bothered by _confined_ spaces?

3. What are some polite things you can say to someone who is speaking _incoherently_?

4. Do you know of any situations where people have been _exploited_? What should be done in these cases?

5. When you want something, are you _persistent,_ or do you give up easily?

LESSON 2

A. WORD FAMILIES

Study the five word families below. Then fill in the word form chart. The underlined word forms at the top of the list are the most commonly used forms in academic texts.

assurance	collapse (2X)	devote	infrastructure	nuclear
/əˈʃʊrəns/	/kəˈlæps/	/dɪˈvoutɪ/	/ˈɪnfrəˌstrʌktʃər/	/ˈnukliər/
assure	collapsed	devoted		
assured	collapsible	devotedly		
assuredly	collapsing	devotion		
assuring				

Exercise - Word Form Chart

NOUN	VERB	ADJECTIVE	ADVERB
1. assurance	1.	1. 2.	1.
1. collapse	1.	1. 2. 3.	1.
1.	1. devote	1.	1.
1. infrastructure			
		1. nuclear	

B. READING

Nuclear Power: Opposing Sides

Proponents of nuclear energy believe that it is important to reduce dependence on non-renewable energy sources, such as gas and oil. They feel that the development of <u>nuclear</u> power plants is an essential component of a strong national <u>infrastructure</u>, and they offer <u>assurance</u> to the general public that <u>nuclear</u> power is clean and safe. On the other hand, those opposed to <u>nuclear</u> energy argue that nuclear power plants are potentially dangerous. They cite several <u>nuclear</u> disasters around the world where the <u>collapse</u> of the so-called safety mechanisms resulted in death, illness, and long-term danger to the people living in the area. These opponents are <u>devoted</u> to the movement against nuclear power.

C. COMPREHENSION CHECK
Exercise 1
Refer to the reading above and use the context to guess the meanings of the words below. Then match the words to their definitions. Do NOT use a dictionary.

___ 1. nuclear	A.	dedicated, showed great care and concern
___ 2. infrastructure	B.	descent into ruin, loss of strength to hold up
___ 3. assurance	C.	related to a nucleus or center
___ 4. collapse	D.	guarantee, pledge
___ 5. devoted	E.	basic things that help a country's people and economy

Exercise 2
True or False? Write T or F in the blanks.

___ 1. Good stores offer their customers the <u>assurance</u> that they can get a refund if their purchase is not satisfactory.

___ 2. The atomic bomb is an example of a <u>nuclear</u> weapon.

___ 3. A <u>devoted</u> dog will run away from his owner as soon as he can dig a hole under the fence.

___ 4. A country's <u>infrastructure</u> includes things like electricity and roads.

___ 5. If your business is well run and profitable, it is sure to <u>collapse</u>.

D. WORD STUDY
Exercise
These are some common collocations for the vocabulary words in this lesson.

---

self-assurance - self-confidence

to rest assured - to feel confident that everything is okay

nuclear family - basic family unit consisting of two parents and their children (vs. extended family where other relatives, such as grandparents, aunts, cousins, etc., live with the family)

Write YES if the collocations have been used correctly or NO if they have been used incorrectly.

_____ 1. You can <u>rest assured</u> that the sun will rise in the east and set in the west.

_____ 2. Grandparents often live with their children and grandchildren in a <u>nuclear family</u>.

_____ 3. Being congratulated on his good work by the boss really helped build Andrew's <u>self-assurance</u>.

E. USING WORDS IN COMMUNICATION
Exercise

Work with a partner.

1. List three things you like or dislike about <u>nuclear power</u>.

2. Do you think it's better to live in a <u>nuclear family</u> or an extended family that includes several other relatives? What is the norm in your family?

3. How do you feel about <u>nuclear weapons</u>? Is it good for countries to have them as a deterrent, or should they be banned?

4. What are the most important parts of a country's <u>infrastructure</u> in your opinion?

5. Name and describe three people or causes that you are <u>devoted</u> to.

4. What can you <u>rest assured</u> about? What would you like to have more <u>assurances</u> about?

LESSON 3

A. WORD FAMILIES
Study the five word families below. Then fill in the word form chart. The underlined word forms at the top of the list are the most commonly used forms in academic texts.

commodity	intrinsic	invoke	minimal	qualitative
/kə'madəti/	/ɪn'trɪncɪk/	/ɪn'vouk/	/'mɪnəməl/	/'kwɑlə ˈteɪtɪv/
		intrinsically	minimalist	qualitatively
			minimally	

Exercise - Word Form Chart

NOUN	VERB	ADJECTIVE	ADVERB
1. commodity			
		1. intrinsic	1.
	1. invoke		
1.		1. minimal	1.
		1. qualitative	1.

B. READING

A Marketing Strategy

The use of persuasive techniques is <u>intrinsic</u> to good salesmanship. Even if a customer has only <u>minimal</u> interest in or need for a certain <u>commodity</u>, a good salesperson will use many creative strategies to make the sale. Testimonials from movie stars about the value of the product may be <u>invoked</u>. These clever emotional appeals can cause the consumer to forget about practical and realistic considerations and instead to make a favorable <u>qualitative</u> judgment. Suddenly it seems absolutely essential to purchase the product!

C. COMPREHENSION CHECK
Exercise 1
Refer to the reading above and use the context to guess the meanings of the words below. Then match the words to their definitions. Do NOT use a dictionary.

___ 1. intrinsic	A.	based on feelings or opinions rather than fact
___ 2. minimal	B.	related to the least amount of something
___ 3. commodity	C.	belonging naturally to something, inherent
___ 4. invoked	D.	called upon, used, put into effect
___ 5. qualitative	E.	item or substance for sale

Exercise 2

Fill in the blanks with the vocabulary words from Exercise 1.

1. A decision based on scientific evidence is quantitative, whereas a decision based on emotions is _____ .

2. Searching for a mate is _____ behavior in most animals.

3. A CD of the performer's music is a popular _____ at a concert.

4. During the national emergency, the president _____ special powers that allowed him to make quick decisions without the approval of congress.

5. Jack was so lazy that he only put forth the _____ effort to pass the class.

D. WORD STUDY
Exercise

Some words change in meaning when they change word forms. Look at the example below.

> 1. minimal - related to the smallest amount of something
>
> 2. minimalist - a person who does minimal art, a nonrepresentational form of art that mostly uses basic geometrical forms and shapes

Some words have common collocations. Look at the following examples.

> intrinsic to   intrinsic worth (value, merit)

Fill in the blanks with the letter of the correct word or phrase

1. We gain self-assurance from our sense of _____.

2. The painter made _____ use of black in his painting. He wanted it to be very colorful.

3. Craig's friend is a _____. Craig doesn't understand her art at all, but for some reason he likes it.

4. Making mistakes is _____ learning.

E. USING WORDS IN COMMUNICATION
Exercise

Reread the reading at the beginning of the lesson. Then close your book. Without looking at the reading, give your partner a summary of the reading. Use as many of the vocabulary words as you can.

LESSON 4

A. WORD FAMILIES

Study the five word families below. Then fill in the word form chart. The underlined word forms at the top of the list are the most commonly used forms in academic texts.

procedure	restraint	specify	straightforward	violation
/prə'sidʒər/	/ rɪ'streɪnt/	/ 'spɛsə͵faɪ/	/straɪt'fɔrwərd/	/͵vaɪə'leɪʃən/
proceed	restrain	specifiable		violate
procedural	restrained	specified		violated
proceedings	restraining	unspecified		violator
proceeds	unrestrained			

Exercise - Word Form Chart

NOUN	VERB	ADJECTIVE	ADVERB
1. procedure 2. 3.	1.	1.	
1. restraint	1.	1. 2. 3.	
	1. specify	1. 2. 3.	
		1. straightforward	
1. violation 2.	1.	1.	

B. READING

Following the Law

When the police decide to make an arrest, the procedure they have been trained to follow is very straightforward. First of all, restraints, such as handcuffs, can be used to detain the suspect, but only the minimal amount of force necessary should be used in making the arrest. The police should exercise restraint and avoid angry or emotional outbursts. Then the suspect must be read his or her rights. The police must specify that the suspect has the right to remain silent and the right to seek legal representation. It is a serious violation of the rules to not read these rights to the suspect.

C. COMPREHENSION CHECK

Exercise 1

Refer to the reading above and use the context to guess the meanings of the words below. Then match the words to their definitions. Do NOT use a dictionary.

___ 1.	procedure	A.	an act of breaking a law or rule
___ 2.	straightforward	B.	things that hold or restrict movement
___ 3.	restraints	C.	say or communicate exactly
___ 4.	violation	D.	clear, direct, without complications
___ 5.	specify	E.	a detailed method of doing something

Exercise 2
Write YES if the underlined word is used correctly or NO if the word is used incorrectly.

_____ 1. The directions to her house were confusing because the distances weren't <u>specified</u>.

_____ 2. Sergeant Hill was given a special award for his well-publicized <u>violation</u>.

_____ 3. Seatbelts are required <u>restraints</u> in all automobiles.

_____ 4. Getting to the main office from here is easy. Just walk <u>straightforward</u>, and you can't miss it!

_____ 5. Renewing a driver's license is a simple <u>procedure</u>. You can even do it by mail or on the computer.

_____ 6. Although he was very angry, he used <u>restraint</u> and tried to speak calmly to the disobedient child.

D. WORD STUDY
Exercise
Some words change in meaning as they change word form. Look at the following examples. Then do the exercise that follows.

---

1. procedure (n) and procedural (adj) - referring to a detailed method of doing something

2. proceed (v) - to continue or resume an activity in progress

3. proceeds (n) - refers to the financial profit from the sale of something

4. proceedings (n) - a noun that means the formal actions in a courtroom during a trial

---

Match the clauses on the left with those that complete them on the right. Write the letters of the completions in the blanks.

___ 1. As soon as the fire drill is finished,   A. during the high security <u>proceedings</u>.

___ 2. If our bake sale is a big success,   B. you will have to follow a long, complex <u>procedure</u>.

___ 3. No one was allowed to enter the courtroom   C. we can use the <u>proceeds</u> to furnish the meeting room.

___ 4. If you want to immigrate to the U.S.,   D. you may <u>proceed</u> with your work.

E. USING WORDS IN COMMUNICATION

Exercise

Write down a **straightforward procedure** for doing something. Be sure to **specify** each step clearly. Compare with a partner and decide which one has the most coherent set of directions.

REVIEW

Choose one word from the list on the right to complete each sentence. Write the word in the blank. Do not use the same word twice.

1. Clarity and logic is _____.   A. assurance

2. To keep within limits is to _____.   B. collapsing

3. A feeling of sadness is _____.   C. commodity

4. A guarantee or pledge is an _____.   D. confine

5. Inherent is _____.   E. depression

6. The least amount is _____.   F. devote

7. To call upon or use is to _____.   G. exploitation

8. Clear and direct is _____.   H. coherence

9. Things that hold are _____.   I. infrastructure

10. Continuing, not stopping is _____.   J. intrinsic

11. Something for sale is a _____.   K. invoke

12. A detailed method is a _____.   L. minimal

13. Based on feelings is _____.   M. nuclear

14. Breaking a law is a _____.   N. persistent

15. Falling down is _____.   O. procedure

16. To state exactly is to _____.   P. qualitative

17. To dedicate is to _____.   Q. restraints

18. Unfair treatment is _____.   R. specify

19. The foundation of a country is_____.   S. straightforward

20. Related to a center or nucleus is _____.   T. violation

UNIT 7

WORDS

albeit	distort	mutual	route
complement	implicit	notwithstanding	scenario
conceive	inclination	offset	suspend
concurrent	integral	practitioner	trigger
controversy	mediate	protocol	whereby

READINGS

Transportation Troubles
Small Claims Court
Character Development
Doctor's Orders

STRATEGIES AND SKILLS

Word Forms
- Word family chart
- Word form selection

Comprehension Check
- Matching definitions
- Understanding and using words in context
- Identifying synonyms

Word Expansion
- Multiple meaning
- Spelling comparison
- Collocations

Interactive Speaking Practice
- Listing
- Associations
- Discussion
- Role Play

ACADEMIC WORD POWER

LESSON 1

A. WORD FAMILIES

Study the five word families below. Then fill in the word form chart. The underlined word forms at the top of the list are the most commonly used forms in academic texts.

concurrent	conceive	implicit	mutual	notwithstanding
/kənˈkɛrənt	/kənˈsiv/	/ɪmˈplɪsɪt/	/ˈmyuʃuəl/	/ˌnɑtwɪθˈstændɪŋ/
concurrently	conceivable	implicitly	mutually	
concur	conceivably			
concurrence	inconceivable			

Exercise - Word Form Chart

NOUN	VERB	ADJECTIVE	ADVERB
1.	1.	1. concurrent	1.
	1. conceive	1. 2.	1.
		1. implicit	1.
		1. mutual	1.
			1. notwithstanding

B. READING

Transportation Troubles

   Michele and her cousin Angela shared an apartment and attended the same university. Their first semester was hard on them both because they only had one car but very different class schedules. They had an <u>implicit</u> agreement that whoever had a class at a given time had first use of the car, but as the semester progressed, they had many transportation problems <u>notwithstanding</u>. For their second semester, they <u>conceived</u> a much better plan. They made a <u>mutual</u> agreement to register for <u>concurrent</u> classes so that they could easily share the car on school days.

C. COMPREHENSION CHECK
Exercise 1
Refer to the reading above and use the context to guess the meanings of the words below. Then match the words to their definitions. Do NOT use a dictionary.

____ 1. implicit	A. understood but not directly stated
____ 2. notwithstanding	B. happening at the same time
____ 3. conceived	C. having similar feelings or ideas
____ 4. mutual	D. thought of something
____ 5. concurrent	E. in spite of this

Exercise 2

Write YES if the underlined word is used correctly and NO if it is used incorrectly.

_____ 1. I was tired, so I decided to cancel the meeting <u>notwithstanding</u>.

_____ 2. Jack and Joshua have a <u>mutual</u> dislike of housework.

_____ 3. The movie was so popular that the movie theater scheduled five <u>concurrent</u> showings.

_____ 4. Every day the teacher told us to speak only English in class. She made this rule very <u>implicit</u>.

_____ 5. An innovative plan for flexible working hours was <u>conceived</u> by the staff.

D. WORD STUDY
Exercise

Study the multiple uses and meanings for the vocabulary words, and then do the exercise that follows.

---

1. concurrent (adj) - happening at the same time

2. concurrent (adj) - having the same opinion

---

3. conceive (v) - think of something

4. conceive (v) - become pregnant

5. (in)conceivable (adj) - (not) imaginable, possible, believable

---

6. mutual (adj) - having similar feelings, ideas, tastes

7. mutual (adj) - sharing business or other interests

---

8. notwithstanding (adv) - in spite of this, nevertheless

9. notwithstanding (prep) - in spite of

Match the clauses on the left with those on the right that complete the sentences. Write the letters of the completions in the blanks.

___ 1. After the couple had been
     married for 15 years,

A. notwithstanding, we will
    deliver the furniture.

___ 2. They tried to be supportive
     of their son's dream

B. due to the concurrent views
    of the committee members.

___ 3. He won the race

C. that airline offered several
    concurrent flights to Seattle.

___ 4. Kim and Lance bought
     the restaurant together,

D. their daughter was conceived.

___ 5. The new resolution was
     easily passed

E. even though they found most
    of his vision inconceivable.

___ 6. It looks like it's going to
     rain hard;

F. his injury notwithstanding.

___ 7. Due to the heavy holiday
     traffic,

G. so they have a mutual interest in
    its success.

E. USING WORDS IN COMMUNICATION
Exercise

1. List three goals that you consider to be conceivable for yourself. Do you know someone who has what you consider to be inconceivable goals?

2. List three mutual interests that you and a friend share.

3. When is it better to have an implicit agreement rather than a directly stated one?

4. When do you think you will have mastered all the vocabulary in this book, the difficulty of the task notwithstanding?

LESSON 2

A. WORD FAMILIES

Study the five word families below. Then fill in the word form chart. The underlined word forms at the top of the list are the most commonly used forms in academic texts.

controversy	distort	mediate	suspend	trigger (2X)
/'kɑntrə ˌvɛrsi/	/dɪ'sɔrtɪd/	/'midi ˌeɪt/	/sə'spɛnd/	/'trɪgər/
controversial	distortion	mediation	suspended	triggered
controversially	distorted	mediating	suspending	triggering
uncontroversial	distorting	mediated	suspension	

Exercise - Word Form Chart

NOUN	VERB	ADJECTIVE	ADVERB
1. controversy		1. 2.	1.
1.	1. distort	1. 2.	
1.	1. mediate	1. 2.	
1.	1. suspend	1. 2.	
1.	1. trigger	1. 2.	

B. READING

Small Claims Court

Small claims court is a division of the legal system set up to deal with lawsuits involving only a few thousand dollars. Small claims cases often deal with some kind of <u>controversy</u> between neighbors or family members, or perhaps between a tenant and landlord. It is generally recommended that the disputing sides try to settle their disagreement out of court first. The two sides meet with someone who can <u>mediate</u> their negotiations and hopefully lead them to a mutually acceptable agreement. However, if this doesn't work, the two sides then take their case to court. The judge listens to both sides and attempts to discern when people give factual accounts and when they tend to <u>distort</u> the information. Sometimes the emotional accusations <u>trigger</u> an angry outburst or even a fist fight. At this point, the judge may <u>suspend</u> the trial and order both parties to seek counseling before returning to the courtroom.

C. COMPREHENSION CHECK
Exercise 1
Refer to the preceding reading and use the context to guess the meanings of the words below. Then match the words to their definitions. Do NOT use a dictionary.

___ 1. controversy   A. help both sides in reaching an agreement
___ 2. mediate   B. twisted, misrepresented
___ 3. distorted   C. start a reaction
___ 4. trigger   D. stop or delay for a period of time
___ 5. suspend   E. public disagreement, usually involving strong opinions

Exercise 2
Circle the word that does not belong.

1. disagreement	controversy	opposition	harmony
2. distorted	distanced	misrepresented	twisted
3. negotiate	go between	mediate	medicate
4. encourage	suspend	delay	stop
5. instigate	control	trigger	start

D. WORD STUDY
Exercise
Study the multiple uses and meanings for the vocabulary words, and then do the exercise that follows.

1. suspend (v) - to stop or delay for a period of time, interrupt, postpone

2. suspend (v) - to hang from a point so as to allow free movement

3. suspend (v) - to take away someone's right to belong to or participate in a group or to enjoy certain privileges, especially because of misbehavior, failure to pay dues, violation of rules, etc.

4. suspend (v) - to support or keep from falling without apparent attachment, as by buoyancy (like floating in water)

5. trigger (v) - to start a reaction

6. trigger (v) - to start an explosion

7. trigger (n) - a lever used to fire a gun

8. trigger (n) - any device or event used to set something off

Write the number from the above list that corresponds to the way the vocabulary word is used in each of the following sentences.

___ 1. A law has been proposed requiring a safety lock on all guns so that children can't accidentally pull the <u>trigger</u>.

___ 2. When soup is cooked, fat always rises to the surface, and this <u>suspended</u> mass can easily be removed with a spoon.

___ 3. Amy's comment about the speech was the <u>trigger</u> for an hour long discussion.

___ 4. Craig was <u>suspended</u> from the football team for smoking in the locker room.

___ 5. The bank robber <u>triggered</u> the explosives and blew up the door to the vault.

___ 6. The artist's sculpture was <u>suspended</u> from the ceiling and seemed to be flying.

___ 7. The restaurant will <u>suspend</u> its business for one month while it is being redecorated.

___ 8. The comedian's joke <u>triggered</u> three full minutes of laughter from the audience.

E. USING WORDS IN COMMUNICATION
Exercise

Associations - On a separate piece of paper, make five lists using the vocabulary words from this lesson. In each list, write at least five words you associate with the vocabulary word. Then cut up the lists and see if your partner can put the lists back together again. Discuss why you chose the associations.

LESSON 3

A. WORD FAMILIES
Study the five word families below. Then fill in the word form chart. The underlined word forms at the top of the list are the most commonly used forms in academic texts.

complement (2X)	integral	offset	scenario	whereby
/ ˈkɑmpləmənt	/ˈɪntəgrəl/	/ˈɔfˌsɛt/	/ səˈnɛriˌ oʊ/	/ wɛrˈbaɪ/
complementary				

Exercise - Word Form Chart

NOUN	VERB	ADJECTIVE	ADVERB
1. complement	1.	1.	
		1. integral	
	1. offset		
1. scenario			
			1. whereby

B. READING

Character Development

In addition to a clear description of the <u>scenario</u>, the events surrounding the plot line, strong character development is <u>integral</u> to the writing of a good story. Adding an indication of what the characters are thinking as a <u>complement</u> to what they are actually saying to each other is one way to add more depth to their personalities. Moreover, the addition of new, secondary characters as the story develops can <u>offset</u> too much direct focus on the main characters while setting up interactions <u>whereby</u> the main characters reveal even more about themselves.

C. COMPREHENSION CHECK
Exercise 1
Refer to the reading above and use the context to guess the meanings of the words below. Then match the words to their definitions. Do NOT use a dictionary.

___ 1. scenario	A.	to balance, compensate for
___ 2. integral	B.	by means of which, through which
___ 3. complement	C.	necessary, essential
___ 4. offset	D.	useful, appropriate addition to something
___ 5. whereby	E.	description of general events that make up a general situation

Exercise 2
Write T for true or F for false.

_____ 1. A <u>scenario</u> can include things that happened just before the story begins.
_____ 2. Getting an "A" on the second test can <u>offset</u> a low score on the first test.
_____ 3. Income taxation is a system <u>whereby</u> citizens contribute to maintaining the infrastructure of the country.
_____ 4. Candy is an <u>integral</u> part of a nutritional diet.
_____ 5. Many people believe that white wine is a good <u>complement</u> to a fish dinner.

D. WORD STUDY
Exercise 1
Sometimes words can be easily confused with other words that have a similar spelling and pronunciation. Study the differences between **complement** and **compliment**.

---

1. complement (n) - a useful addition to something

2. complement (v) - to be a useful or appropriate addition that makes something more effective or complete

3. complementary (adj) - serving to fill out or complete

4. complementary (adj) - mutually supplying each other's lack or needs

---

5. compliment (n) - an expression of admiration, praise, or congratulations

6. compliment (v) - to express praise or admiration to someone

7. complimentary (adj) - expressing praise, admiring

8. complimentary (adj) - free, without charge

Write your own sentences on the lines below that demonstrate your understanding of the meanings of **complement/complementary** .

(complement – noun)
1. _____

(complement – verb)
2. _____

(complementary – adjective)
3. _____

4. _____

Exercise 2

Some words are commonly used with other words. Study the collocations below, and then do the exercise that follows.

---

worst case **scenario** - the worst thing you can imagine happening

complementary colors - colors that are located directly across from each other on the color wheel (red-green, blue-orange, purple-yellow) that contrast because they share no common colors

---

1. Think of a problem you have right now and imagine the <u>worst case scenario</u>. Now think of the <u>best case scenario</u>. Which one do you think is more probable?

2. Which pair of <u>complementary colors</u> do you like least? Why do you think an artist might use <u>complementary colors</u> together in a painting?

E. USING WORDS IN COMMUNICATION

Exercise

Discuss the following in small groups.

1. What components are <u>integral</u> to a good job? Rank them according to their importance to you as a single person. Then rank them as a married person with five children. Are your lists similar or different? Why?

2. Do you think your good qualities <u>offset</u> your bad qualities? Explain.

3. Imagine you are going to redecorate your living room. What main color would choose? What other colors would you use to <u>complement</u> the main color? What decoration would you add to your room to <u>complement</u> the basic furniture?

LESSON 4

A. WORD FAMILIES

Study the five word families below. Then fill in the word form chart. The underlined word forms at the top of the list are the most commonly used forms in academic texts.

albeit	inclination	practitioner	protocol	route (2X)
/ɔl'biət/	/ɪnklə'neɪʃən/	/ præk'tɪʃənər/	/ 'prutə͜ kɔl/	/raut/ or /rut/
	incline (2X)			routed
	inclined			

Exercise - Word Form Chart

NOUN	VERB	ADJECTIVE	CONJUNCTION
			1. albeit
1. inclination 2.	1.	1.	
1. practitioner			
1. protocol			
1. route	1.	1.	

B. READING

Doctor's Orders

When doctors and other health care professionals get their medical licenses, they promise to follow a strict code of ethics concerning patient care. They also must agree to follow certain rules of medical procedure. There are times when a medical <u>practitioner</u> has a strong <u>inclination</u> to go against standard <u>protocol</u> and follow an alternate <u>route</u> in treating a patient's illness, perhaps even trying out a new drug or treatment that has not yet been officially approved. This desire, <u>albeit</u> coming from sincere concern for the patients recovery, if followed, could lead to suspension of the right to practice medicine.

C. COMPREHENSION CHECK
Exercise 1

Refer to the reading above and use the context to guess the meanings of the words below. Then match the words to their definitions. Do NOT use a dictionary.

___ 1. practitioner		A.	even though, despite
___ 2. inclination		B.	a path along which one proceeds
___ 3. protocol		C.	preference, leaning, desire to do something
___ 4. route		D.	a person who does skilled work
___ 5. albeit		E.	acceptable practices or rules of behavior in a profession.

Exercise 2

Fill in the blanks with one of the vocabulary words for this lesson.

1. It is possible, _____ difficult, to climb that mountain in 10 hours.

2. Lucas had a strong _____ to eat sweets.

3. We can either take the scenic _____ or the direct highway home.

4. One must follow specific _____ when greeting royalty.

5. A dental _____ is trained to detect tooth decay.

D. WORD STUDY
Exercise

Some words have more than one meaning or usage. Study the multiple meanings of the words below, and then do the exercise that follows.

1. inclination (n) - preference, leaning, desire to do something

2. incline (n) - a hill or slope, usually of land

3. incline (v) - to tilt at an angle

4. incline (v) - to bend forward or backward

5. inclined (adj) - preferring, likely to

6. inclined (adj) - slanted, tilted

7. route (n) - a path along which one travels

8. route (n) - a series of stops made regularly by someone who delivers things

9. route (v) - to tell someone to go a certain way

Write YES if the underlined word is used correctly or NO if it is used incorrectly.

_____ 1. Traffic was <u>routed</u> onto a side road because of the big parade.

_____ 2. The children raced their sleds down the snowy <u>incline</u>.

_____ 3. Paul <u>inclines</u> to be late for meetings.

_____ 4. The postal worker usually finishes her <u>route</u> by 4:00.

_____ 5. The <u>inclination</u> of that mountain was too steep to climb without equipment.

_____ 6. Wendy <u>inclined</u> her head to see around the tall man seated in front of her.

E. USING WORDS IN COMMUNICATION
Exercise

Role Play - Find a partner. One of you will be a medical **practitioner** (doctor, dentist, nurse, etc) and the other will be a demanding patient. Create a scenario in which the patient wants the practitioner to go against **protocol** and provide unapproved medication or treatment. The medical practitioner has to resist any inclination to give in to the patient and must convince the patient to follow the traditional, **albeit** lengthy, **route** to recovery.

REVIEW

Use words from the list at the beginning of this unit to fill in the blanks. Then add the words to the puzzle on the following page.

ACROSS

1. One must follow diplomatic _____ when a foreign dignitary arrives at the airport.
3. We cannot give you a scholarship, your excellent grades _____ .
4. Although unspoken, their loyalty to each other was _____ .
7. Instead of driving home the usual way, we decided to take an alternate_____ .
9. Elaine hates to argue, so she avoids all _____ .
12. A necklace can be a nice _____ to a plain dress.
14. This task, _____ difficult, is not impossible.
15. The reunion of a group of old friends was the _____ for the story.
16. Most elementary schools have a free breakfast program _____ children from low-income families can get a nutritious and free breakfast every morning.

DOWN

2. Our presentations are at _____ times, so you won't be able to see both.
4. Vegetables are an _____ part of a healthy diet.
5. Bethany _____ the truth a little to make it seem that she was not guilty.
6. A thoughtless comment can _____ an angry discussion.
8. We served a bowl of cucumbers and yogurt to _____ the spiciness of the curry.
10. A cardiologist is a kind of medical _____ .
11. The counselor tried to _____ the dispute between the angry neighbors.
12. Whoever _____ the plan for this building must be crazy! There aren't any doors!
13. Our feelings about tests are _____ . We both hate them!

APPENDICES

A. ACADEMIC WORD LIST INDEX
B. ROOTS, PREFIXES, SUFFIXES

APPENDIX A
WORD LIST INDEX

Academic Word List Index

The 140 target words studied in this book come from the Academic Word List (see Introduction, page ix for a description of the AWL). The four volumes of Academic Word Power cover 560 of the 570 words on the AWL. Below is a complete, alphabetical list of the AWL. The numbers indicate the volume, unit and page number where the word is introduced.

Word	v.u.pg	Word	v.u.pg	Word	v.u.pg
abandon	3.7.90	aspect	1.5.65	coincide	4.4.51
abstract	3.3.40	assemble	4.2.18	collapse	4.6.78
academy	2.2.18	assess	1.6.85	colleague	4.1.2
access	2.7.92	assign	3.7.101	commence	4.5.64
accommodate	4.5.70	assist	1.1.8	comment	3.7.96
accompany	3.7.101	assume	3.1.5	commission	1.6.76
accumulate	4.1.8	assure	4.6.78	commitment	2.5.75
accurate	2.7.94	attach	2.6.89	commodity	4.6.81
achieve	1.2.18	attain	4.2.24	communicate	
acknowledge	3.4.46	attitude	2.2.21	community	1.1.2
acquire	1.7.100	attribute	3.1.5	compatible	4.5.60
adapt	3.6.84	author	2.5.75	compensate	2.2.24
adequate	2.6.89	authority	1.4.46	compile	4.5.64
adjacent	4.4.46	automate	3.3.32	complement	4.7.96
adjust	2.5.66	available	1.1.8	complex	1.4.53
administrate	1.4.46	aware	2.4.56	component	4.1.11
adult	3.2.24	behalf	4.5.70	compound	4.3.35
advocate	3.4.46	benefit	1.1.8	comprehensive	3.4.49
affect	1.2.18	bias	3.3.34	comprise	3.5.66
aggregate	3.5.60	bond	4.1.2	compute	1.4.56
aid	3.2.24	brief	2.5.69	conceive	4.7.90
albeit	4.7.99	bulk	4.3.32	concentrate	2.7.94
allocate	3.6.81	capable	3.2.18	concept	1.3.41
alter	2.1.8	capacity	2.6.86	conclude	1.1.11
alternative	2.3.37	category	1.5.71	concurrent	4.7.90
ambiguous	3.4.52	cease	4.4.46	conduct	1.7.90
amend	3.1.8	challenge	2.1.5	confer	4.1.11
analogy	4.4.48	channel	4.1.8	confine	4.6.76
analyze	1.5.68	chapter	1.2.18	confirm	3.3.32
annual	2.1.11	chart	4.3.40	conflict	3.1.2
anticipate	4.1.11	chemical	4.2.18	conform	3.4.52
apparent	2.4.60	circumstance	2.2.21	consent	2.7.100
append	4.3.32	cite	3.4.46	consequent	1.7.93
appreciate	3.2.24	civil	2.5.69	considerable	2.4.50
approach	1.2.18	clarify	3.6.81	consist	1.4.46
appropriate	1.3.32	classic	4.3.32	constitute	
approximate	2.2.28	clause	2.4.60	constant	2.3.43
arbitrary	4.3.38	code	4.2.21	contract	1.5.71
area	1.1.11	coherent	4.6.76	constrain	3.1.8

Word	v.u.pg	Word	v.u.pg	Word	v.u.pg
constrain	1.6	differentiate	3.6.74	evaluate	1.2.21
consult	2.6.86	dimension	2.6.86	eventual	3.4.52
consume	1.3.32	diminish	4.3.35	evident	1.3.38
contact	4.3.32	discrete	2.7.100	evolve	2.4.57
contemporary	3.3.34	discriminate	3.4.52	exceed	3.3.32
context	1.218	displace	4.5.70	exclude	1.7.90
contradict	3.5.66	display	2.5.75	exhibit	3.7.97
contrary	4.2.21	dispose	3.6.77	expand	4.3.40
contrast	2.2.24	distinct	1.4.50	expert	2.6.83
contribute	2.3.40	distort	4.7.93	explicit	3.5.63
controversy	4.7.93	distribute	1.5.68	exploit	4.6.76
convene	2.5.75	diverse	3.3.34	export	1.5.71
converse	4.1.2	document	1.7.93	external	2.3.46
convert	3.6.84	domain	3.5.60	extract	3.6.77
convince	4.4.46	domestic	2.4.53	facilitate	4.3.32
cooperate	3.2.27	dominate	2.3.37	factor	1.1.2
coordinate	2.2.94	draft	2.6.86	feature	1.4.50
core	1.7.100	drama	3.7.90	federal	4.2.27
corporate	4.2.24	duration	4.2.27	fee	2.5.66
correspond	2.3.43	dynamic	3.4.55	file	4.1.5
couple		economy	1.4.50	final	1.1.14
create	1.2.21	edit	3.5.69	finance	1.5.62
credit	1.3.32	element	1.3.41	finite	3.6.77
criteria	2.7.104	eliminate	3.2.21	flexible	2.5.75
crucial	3.4.49	emerge	2.3.34	fluctuate	3.7.97
culture	1.1.2	emphasis	1.2.21	focus	1.3.32
currency	4.4.54	empirical	3.6.74	format	4.4.51
cycle	2.2.21	enable	4.1.5	formula	1.7.100
data	1.3.35	encounter	4.3.40	forthcoming	4.5.84
debate	2.2.18	energy	2.1.2	foundation	3.3.37
decade	3.2.21	enforce	3.1.2	found	4.3.40
decline	2.4.50	enhance	3.3.34	framework	2.2.28
deduce	2.2.28	enormous	4.4.54	function	1.5.68
define	1.1.11	ensure	2.1.5	fund	1.7.93
definite	3.6.77	entity	4.2.18	fundamental	2.3.37
demonstrate	2.1.5	environment	1.1.5	furthermore	2.6.89
denote	4.2.27	equate	1.6.82	gender	3.2.18
deny	3.2.18	equip	3.2.21	generate	3.1.11
depress	4.6.76	equivalent	2.5.72	generation	2.2.28
derived	3.1.5	erode	4.4.46	globe	3.3.34
design	1.3.35	error	2.2.24	goal	2.1.8
despite	2.1.8	establish	1.6.79	grade	4.2.21
detect	3.7.94	estate		grant	2.4.57
deviate	4.4.51	estimate	1.5.62	guarantee	3.2.18
device	4.5.64	ethic	4.3.40	guideline	3.3.32
devoted	4.6.78	ethnic	2.4.53	hence	4.1.8

Word	v.u.pg	Word	v.u.pg	Word	v.u.pg
phase	2.2.28	recover	3.1.10	simulate	3.4.55
phenomenon	3.4.55	refine	4.5.67	site	1.7.90
philosophy	1.7.96	regime	4.2.27	so-called	4.5.67
physical	1.1.5	region	1.3.41	sole	3.2.18
plus	4.2.24	register	1.7.96	somewhat	3.4.52
policy	1.3.41	regulate	1.5.65	source	2.1.2
portion	4.3.35	reinforce	3.7.101	specific	1.4.53
pose	4.5.67	reject	2.3.34	specify	4.6.84
positive	1.3.32	relax	4.1.5	sphere	4.2.24
potential	1.6.76	release	3.5.60	stable	2.5.66
practitioner	4.7.99	relevant	1.6.82	statistic	2.5.72
precede	3.3.40	reluctance	4.3.38	status	2.6.80
precise	2.6.80	rely	1.4.50	straightforward	4.6.84
predict	2.1.5	remove	1.4.56	strategy	1.5.62
predominant	3.7.90	require	1.2.27	stress	2.1.2
preliminary	4.4.51	research	1.4.53	structure	1.4.56
presume	3.4.49	reside	1.5.65	style	2.3.37
previous	1.4.46	resolve	2.4.50	submit	3.6.81
primary	1.5.71	resource	1.4.53	subordinate	4.5.60
prime	2.6.80	restrain	4.6.84	subsequent	2.7.100
principal	2.7.94	restrict	1.7.93	subsidy	3.5.66
principle	1.4.56	retain	2.7.97	substitute	2.6.89
prior	3.3.37	reveal	3.1.5	successor	3.3.40
proceed	4.6.84	revenue	2.6.89	sufficient	2.4.57
process	1.2.24	reverse	3.5.63	sum	2.3.40
professional	2.1.2	revise	3.6.81	summary	2.7.104
prohibit	3.5.63	revolution	4.4.48	supplement	4.4.54
project	2.3.34	revise	3.6.81	survey	1.3.35
promote	2.7.97	role	1.6.76	survive	3.5.69
proportion	2.4.53	route	4.7.99	suspend	4.7.93
prospect	3.6.84	scenario	4.7.96	sustain	2.3.34
protocol	4.7.99	schedule	3.2.27	symbol	2.4.60
psychology		scheme	2.7.100	tape	4.1.5
publication	3.5.66	scope	3.6.81	target	2.1.11
publish	2.2.18	section	1.2.27	task	1.2.27
purchase	1.5.62	sector	1.6.85	team	4.2.24
pursue	2.5.69	secure	1.3.38	technical	4.1.8
qualitative	4.6.81	seek	1.6.82	technique	1.7.90
quote	3.3.37	select	1.3.35	technology	1.3.38
radical	3.7.90	sequence	1.7.100	temporary	4.3.38
random	3.2.27	sex		tense	3.4.46
range	1.6.79	series	2.1.8	terminate	3.6.84
ratio	3.1.8	shift	2.7.100	text	1.3.35
rational	3.4.49	significance	1.3.41	theme	3.7.94
react	1.6.85	similar	1.1.11	theory	1.6.79

Word	v.u.pg
thereby	3.7.101
thesis	3.2.27
topic	3.5.69
trace	3.6.77
tradition	1.2.27
transfer	1.5.68
transform	3.4.55
transit	2.3.43
transmit	3.5.63
transport	3.1.11
trend	2.6.83
trigger	4.7.93
ultimate	3.5.63
undergo	4.4.48
underlie	3.1.2
undertake	2.7.94
uniform	3.7.97
unify	4.5.67
unique	3.3.40
utilize	3.1.11
valid	2.2.18
vary	1.2.27
vehicle	3.7.94
version	2.4.53
via	3.7.94
violate	4.6.84
virtual	3.7.97
visible	3.5.80
vision	4.5.67
visual	4.1.8
volume	2.7.97
voluntary	3.5.69
welfare	2.6.83
whereas	4.1.11
whereby	4.7.96
widespread	3.4.49

APPENDIX B
ROOTS, PREFIXES, SUFFIXES

COMMON ROOTS, PREFIXES AND SUFFIXES IN ACADEMIC VOCABULARY

Academic vocabulary is mainly of Latin or Greek origin, so knowing common Greek and Latin roots, prefixes, and suffixes can be very helpful in learning and remembering academic vocabulary. The following tables list some common roots and affixes along with their meanings and examples. The examples in bold are words from the Academic Word List.

LATIN ROOTS

Roots	Meaning	Examples
act	to do, drive	**interact, compact, extract**
ann, enn	year	**annual,** bicentennial
aqu	water	aquarium, aqueduct
aud	to hear	auditorium, auditor
bell	war	belligerent, bellicose
cede	to go, to yield	**precede,** concede
cent	one hundred	**percent,** centennial
cept, capt, cip, cap, ceive, ceipt	to take hold, grasp	**conceive,** receive, capture
cert	to be sure, to trust	certain, certify
cess, ced	to go, to yield	**process,** successor, cessation
cid, cis	to cut off, be brief, to kill	concise, homicide
circ, circum	around	**circumstance,** circumference
clin	to lean, lie, bend	**decline, incline**
cog	to think, consider	recognize, cognitive
cor, cord, card	heart	coronary, cardiology
corp	body	**corporate,** corpse
cred	to believe, to trust	**credit,** credible
crit, cris	to separate, judge	**criteria** , criticism
culp	fault, blame	culprit, culpable
dic, dict	to say, to speak, to assert	**contradict, predict**
duct, duc	to lead, to draw	**conduct, deduce**
dur	hard, lasting	**duration,** durable
ego	I	egotistical, egocentric
equ	equal, fair	**equation,** equator
fac, fic, fect, fact	to make, do	**facilitate, affect**
fer	to carry, bear, bring	**transfer, infer, confer**
fin	end, limit	**definite, finite, confine**
flu	to flow	**fluctuations,** fluid
form	shape	**uniform** , formula, **transform**
fort	strong	fortify, fortress
fum	smoke, scent	perfume, fumigate
gen	race, family, kind	**generation, gender**
grad, gress	step, degree, rank	**grade,** gradual
grat	pleasing, thankful	grateful, congratulate
grav, griev	heavy	gravity, grieve, grave
hab	to have, hold, to dwell	habitat, habit
hom	man, human	homicide, homage
init	to begin, enter upon	**initial, initiate**
jur, jus, judic	law, right, judgment	**justify, adjust,** judicial
juven	young	juvenile, rejuvenate
laud	praise	laud, laudable
leg	law	**legal, legislate**
liber	free	**liberal, liberate**

Roots	Meaning	Examples
loc	place	**location, allocate,** local
manu	hand	**manual,** manuscript
med, medi	middle	**medium, mediate,** mediocre
medic	physician, to heal	**medical,** medicine
memor	mindful	memorial, memorable
mon	to remind, advise, warn	**monitor, demonstrate**
ment	mind	**mental,** mentality
migr	to move, travel	**immigration, migration**
mit, mis	to send	**transmit,** submit
mort	death	mortal, mortality
mov, mob, mot	to move	**remove,** mobile, motion
mut	change, exchange	mutate, mutant
nomen, nomin	name, meaning	nominate, synonym
null, nihil, nil	nothing, void	nihilism, nullify
ped	foot	pedestrian, pedestal
pend, pond, pens	to weigh, pay, to consider	**compensate,** pension, pensive
plur, plus	more	**plus,** surplus
port	to carry	**export, transport**
pos	to place, put	**dispose, impose, expose**
pot	powerful	**potential,** potent
prim, prin	first	**primary, prime**
reg, rig, rect	to rule, right, straight	**regulation,** rigid
rupt	to break, burst	disrupt, interrupt, rupture
sacr, secr, sanct	sacred	sacrifice, sanctify
sat, satis	enough	satisfy, satiate
scrib, script	to write	inscribe, subscription
sed, sid, sess	to sit, to settle	sedate, sediment, subside
sent, sens	to feel	sentimental, sense
sequ, secut	to follow, sequence	**consequence, sequence, subsequent**
sumil, simul, sembl	like,	**similar, simulation**
sol, soli	alone, lonely	**solely, isolate**
spec, spect, spic	to see, look at, behold	**perspective, inspect**
spond, spons	to pledge, promise	**respond, correspond**
tac, tic	silent	tacit, taciturn
ten, tain, tent	to hold	**obtain, retain, attain**
tend, tens	to stretch, strive	**tension,** tendon
termin	boundary, limit	**terminate, terminal**
test	to witness, affirm	attest, testify
tract	to pull, draw	**contract, extract**
trib	to allot, give	**distribute, contribute**
vac	empty	evacuate, vacuous
ven, vent	to come	**convention, intervene**
ver	truth	verify, veracity
vers, vert	to turn	**convert, reverse, controversy**
via	way, road	**via,** viaduct
vir	manliness, worth	virile, virtue
vis, vid	to see, look	**visible, revision, visual**
viv, vit	life	vital, vivacious
voc, vok	voice, call	**invoke, vocal, revoke**

Roots	Meaning	Examples
GREEK ROOTS		
anthropo	human being	anthropology, philanthropic
aster, astro	star	asteroid, astronomy
bio	life	biography, biology
chrom	color	chromatic, chromosome
chrono	time	chronology, chronometer
cosmo	world, order, universe	cosmos, cosmopolitan
crac, crat	rule, govern	aristocrat, democracy
dem	people	**demonstrate,** epidemic
derm	skin	dermatology, hypodermic
ethno	nation	ethnic, ethnocentric
eu	good, well	euphoric, euphemism
gam	marriage	monogamy, polygamy
geo	earth	geology, geodynamics
gno, kno	to know	knowledge, diagnostic
graph gram	to write, draw, record	telegraph, telegram
gymno, gymn	athletic	gymnasium, gymnastics
hydro	water	hydrogen, hydroplane
hypno	sleep	hypnosis, hypnotize
hypo	under, below	**hypothesis,** hypodermic
logue, logo	idea, word, speech, reason	**logic, ideological**
meter, metr	measure	**parameters,** metric
micro	small	microscope, microorganism
mim	copy	mimic, mime
mono	one	monogram, monogamy
mor	fool	moron, moronic
morph	form, structure, shape	morphology, metamorphosis
neur, nero	nerve	neural, neurotic
opt	eye	optic, optician
ortho	straight	orthodontist, orthopedics
pan	all	**expansion,** pantheism
path	feeling, disease	sympathy, pathologist
phe	speak, spoken about	prophet, euphemistic
phil, philo	love	**philosophy,** philanthropist
phob	fear	phobia, claustrophobia
phon	sound, voice	telephone, phonograph
photo	light	photosynthesis, photography
pneu	breath	pneumonia, pneumatic
polis, polit	citizen, city, state	political, metropolitan
poly	many	polygamy, polytechnic
pseudo	false	pseudo, pseudonym
psych	mind, soul, spirit	psychic, psychology
pyr	fire	pyromania, pyrotechnic
scope	to see	**scope,** telescope
soph	wise	**philosophy,** sophisticated
sym, syn	together	**symbolic,** synthesize
techn	art, skill	**technical, technology**
tele	at a distance	telescope, telephone
the, them, thet	to place, put	**hypothesis,** epithet
thea, theatr	to see, view	theatre, theatrical
theo	God	**theory,** theology
therm	heat	thermometer, thermal

PREFIXES

Prefix	Meaning	Examples
ab-	from, away from	absent, **abnormal**
ad-	to, motion toward, addition to	**advocate, administrate, adapt**
aero-	air	aerobic, aerospace
a-, an-	without	atonal, anarchy
ante-	before	antecedent, anteroom
anti-	against, opposite, reverse	anti-aircraft, antibiotics
ap-	to, nearness to	**approximate**, appoint
auto-	self	**automatic**, autograph
bene-	good	**benefit**, benefactor
bi-	two	**biannual**, bifocal
co-, con-	together	**community, cooperative, coordination , context**
contra-	against	**contrast, controversy, contradiction**
de-	opposite of, away from, undo	**deduction, decline**
dis-	opposite	**displace, disproportion**
ex-	out, beyond, away from, former	**exclude, export, external**
extra-	outside, beyond, besides	extraordinary, extracurricular
fore-	before	foreword, forecast
hyper-	more than normal, too much	hyperactive, hypersensitive
il-	not	**illegal, illogical**
im-	into	**impact, imply, immigrate**
im-	not	**immature**, imbalance
in-	not	**incapable, indiscreet, inaccurate**
inter-	among, between	**interaction, intervention, interval**
intra-	within	intramural, intrastate
ir-	not	**irrelevant, irrational**
mal-	wrong, bad	malfunction, malpractice
mis-	wrong, bad, no, not	misinterpret, misbehave
non-	not, opposite of	nontraditional, nonconformist
per-	through	**perceive, perspective**
post-	after	postgraduate, postglacial
pre-	before	**precede, previous, preliminary**
pro-	before, for, in support of	**promote**, prologue
pro-	forward	**project, proceed**
re-	back, again	**reassess, recreate, redefine**
retro-	backward	retroactive, retrospect
self-	of the self	self-respect, self-taught
semi-	half, partly	semiformal, semi-circle
sub-	under, beneath	**subordinate**, submarine
sur-	over, above	surcharge, surpass, **survey**
trans-	across, over	**transition, transport**
ultra-	extremely	ultramodern, ultrasonic
un-	not, lack of, opposite	**uninvolved, unreliable, unaware**

SUFFIXES

Suffix	Meaning	Examples
-able, -ible	can, able to	detectable, accessible, flexible
-age	action or process	percentage, linkage, voyage
-al, -ial	of, like, relating to, suitable for	cultural, traditional, potential
-ance	act, process, quality, state of being	maintenance, reliance, assurance
-ant	one who	assistant, participant
-ary	of, like, relating to	temporary, primary, voluntary
-ate	characteristic of, to become	alternate, demonstrate, eliminate
-cle, -icle	small	particle, cubicle
-cy	fact, or state of being	policy, residency
-dom	state or quality of	random, boredom
-ence	act or state of being	evidence, sequence, intelligence
-ent	doing, having, showing	consistent, sufficient, inherent
-er	one who, that which	consumer, achiever
-ery	place for, act, practice of	recovery, robbery
-ess	female	princess, goddess
-ful	full of	stressful, insightful
-ic	relating to, characteristic of	economic, specific, academic
-ify	to make, to cause to be	identify, unify
-ion	act, condition, result of,	conclusion, evaluation
-ish	of or belonging to, characterized by	stylish, selfish
-ism	act, practice, or result of, example	individualism, professionalism
-ity	condition, state of being	security, maturity, stability
-ive	of, relating to, belonging to	negative, alternative, legislative
-ize	make, cause to be, subject to	civilize, energize, finalize
-less	without	ceaseless, jobless
-logue	speech	dialogue, monologue
-logy	study or theory of	psychology, ideology
-ly	every	annually, daily
-ly	in (a specified manner, to a specified extent)	normally, automatically
-ment	action or process	commitment, assessment, adjustment
-ment	state or quality of	refinement, amusement
-ment	product or thing	environment, document
-ness	state or quality of being	awareness, uniqueness, intenseness
-or	one who	minor, actor
-ous	having, full of, characterized by	ambiguous, enormous, erroneous
-ship	state or quality of being	partnership, authorship
-some	like, tending to be	bothersome, noisome
-tude	state of quality of being	attitude, solitude
-y	characterized by	contemporary, voluntary, contrary

Reference:
Elliot, Norbert. <u>Vocabulary Workshop</u>. Austin, Texas: Holt, Rinehard and Winston, 2001.